ISNBN: 9798880415595

I.A.O.

"I am the Alpha and the Omega,
The First and the Last,
The Beginning and the End."
(Revelation 22:13)

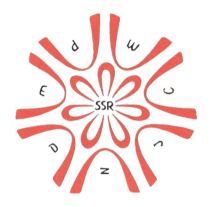

Ex Deo nascimur

In Christo morimur

Per Spiritum Sanctum Reviviscimus

Contents

'I am the Alpha and the Omega, the Beginning and the End," says the Lord, "who is and who was and who is to come, the Almighty.'

John the Apostle

"In the Rosicrucian sense, Christianity is at once the highest development of individual freedom and universal religion. There is a community of free souls. The tyranny of dogma is replaced by the radiance of divine wisdom, embracing intelligence, love, and action. The science that arises from this cannot be measured by its power of abstract reasoning but by its power to bring souls to flower and fruition. That is the difference between 'Logia' and 'Sophia,' between science and divine wisdom, and between Theology and Theosophy. In this sense, Christ is the center of esoteric evolution of the West."

Rudolf Steiner

A Note to the Reader

By studying and contemplating the lectures and quotes of Rudolf Steiner, Paracelsus, and Ita Wegman, as well as the parables of Henricus Madathanus and Christian Rosenkreuz presented in this book, and by practicing Sun Meditation daily, you may find support for your spiritual development. These activities can help develop new skills, improve physical and emotional health, extend life, maintain youthfulness, and assist you in selecting, exploring, and successfully achieving sustainable life goals in harmony with humanity's ascending evolution.

Furthermore, these practices may foster a free and loving connection with spiritual entities such as Christ, Archai Michael, Christian Rosenkreuz, and Rudolf Steiner. It is our hope that this book will strengthen your connection with your Higher Self and Christ in your daily life, aiding in personal and life transformation as a service to humanity.

Please note, the guidance provided in this book is not intended to replace professional advice, treatment, or counseling from registered health professionals or therapists. Meditation and other instructions herein should not be seen as substitutes for any necessary interventions advised by healthcare professionals or therapists. If you suspect you are suffering from a physical or mental illness, it is important to seek professional advice. Always consult a healthcare professional or therapist if in doubt.

About the Author

Dr. Peter Gruenewald, MD, is an anthroposophic doctor and general practitioner with a specialized focus on psychiatry, and behavioral sleep medicine. He is an internationally recognized expert in adaptive resilience, stress management, and performance optimization.

Peter Gruenewald is also a prolific author, contributing significantly to the literature on these topics through several well-regarded books:

"Self-Leadership: Realize Your True Potential" (2023) - This recent publication offers readers insights into harnessing their inner strengths and realizing their full potential through self-guidance and personal growth.

"Mastering Life: Rosicrucian and Magical Techniques for Achieving Your Life's Goals" (Clairview, 2022) - In this book, Gruenewald explores ancient Rosicrucian and magical practices, providing a modern interpretation on how these age-old techniques can be applied to achieve personal and professional goals.

"Manifesting Your Best Future Self: Building Adaptive Resilience" (2020) - This book focuses on developing resilience to adapt and thrive in the face of life's challenges, enhancing one's ability to manifest a positive future.

"The Quiet Heart: Putting Stress into Its Place" (Floris Books, 2007) - Gruenewald offers practical advice on managing stress, aiming to help readers achieve a more peaceful and productive life.

"Gold and the Philosopher's Stone: Treating Chronic Physical and Mental Illness with Mineral Remedies" (Temple Lodge Publishing, May 3, 2002) - This book delves into the use of mineral remedies in treating chronic conditions, drawing on historical and modern perspectives from anthroposophic medicine.

Dr. Gruenewald's works are essential for those interested in the integration of traditional and holistic approaches to health and personal development.

Introduction

Alchemy explores the spiritual science of earthly materials and their interplay with human and cosmic forces. Since the spirit permeates everything, it is inherently present in metals, stones, plants, and animals. Divine intelligence, embodied in love and power, manifests through the light, warmth, and life given by both the inner (human) and outer (astronomical) aspects of the Sun. It is thus not surprising to find these divine qualities in Gold, the most revered of metals, believed to be the ultimate aim of every metal through the process of earthly evolution.

As humans, we must revere the sanctuary of our bodies, Nature, and the Macrocosms as creations of God. By doing so, through the purification of our thoughts, feelings, and deeds, and through our wise, loving, and benevolent interactions with Nature and our fellow human beings, we can 'transmute' lead into gold and transform the human body into the resurrection body of Christ.

Rosicrucian alchemy holds special significance for Christianity; it offers a substantial correction to the erroneous teachings of 'contempt of the flesh' and the anti-cosmological stance held by confessional Christian churches since the late Middle Ages.

In fact, during the early Middle Ages, alchemy was not opposed to Christianity; rather, it could complement Christianity on a physical level. It was not only bread and wine that were transubstantiated, but also minerals, metals, and the lime of bones and rocks. Since the Mystery of Golgotha, Christian alchemists have viewed the Earth as the body of Christ, evolving toward the New Earth of Heavenly Jerusalem.

Alchemy provided cosmological Christianity with a spiritual-scientific and operational practice. Church-based Christianity, however, began to neglect this approach as it aimed not to anchor humanity in the sensory world, but rather to lead it away from it.

Without Christian alchemy, Christianity could not have been 'incarnated'; this absence would create a dual world, dividing the unity of the world into Spirit and Matter. As a result, Earth and Nature would become lost and irredeemable. Furthermore, there would be no perception or acknowledgment of the spirit of Nature, which is vital for enriching science, the arts, and crafts, thereby furthering the evolution of humanity and Earth.

Despite the insistence of historians of science, alchemy was never merely a primitive chemistry, except in its degenerate aspects. It was a 'sacramental' science, where material phenomena were not autonomous but merely representations of the 'condensation' of spiritual realities.

When Nature is penetrated with wise, loving, and benevolent understanding, it becomes transparent. On the one hand, it is transfigured by the lightning flashes of divine forces; on the other, it elevates the Soul to 'angelic' states of consciousness. These states, which fallen man can only glimpse briefly—when listening to music, creating art, contemplating artistic beauty, or engaging with spiritual science, as seen in Goethe's natural science studies, Johannes Kepler's cosmogony, Paracelsus' natural science and theological writings, or Rudolf Steiner's anthroposophy—are profound and fleeting.

In natural processes and their representation through spiritual symbols, God's wisdom, beauty, and power are manifest. These can be deciphered and serve as a foundation for striving toward all-inclusiveness, wholeness, and perfection of the individual, humanity, and Earth in God.

Rosicrucian alchemy acknowledges the unity of man, nature, and the macrocosm. Its task is to research and utilize both the diversity and unity of forces through spiritual science and technology. Inspired by the deeds of Christ, 'spirit-deserted' nature is rejuvenated, becoming once more the body of the 'Creative Word' and, metaphorically, the bride of God.

The physical human body, a creation of nature, can become a matrix for perfection through purification and spiritualization as we foster the resurrection body of Christ within ourselves. By spiritualizing our human constitution and recognizing nature as a condensed spirit, we also redeem nature and elevate it to a higher state of evolution. The transformation of non-precious metals such as lead, iron, or mercury into gold is, in its essence, a spiritual alchemical process. It transmutes the darkness and imperfections of the human soul into its pure solar nature, fully expressing the solar radiance of our higher self in Christ. This transformation also aids in the redemption of nature and Earth through the development of human consciousness and our inspired actions.

Gold is the most perfect of metals, the one whose luminous density best expresses the divine presence of the Holy Trinity in the mineral realm: through spiritual activity, each metal can virtually become Gold, and each stone becomes precious in God. (A detailed description of this process of spiritual alchemy can be found in the chapter about Paracelsus' understanding of the seven metals, the seven planets, and the seven soul and life forces within the human constitution.)

Since the Mystery of Golgotha, the 'Transfiguration of nature-memory' from the paradise of Eden and the anticipated Heavenly Jerusalem of the Revelation of St. John have begun to manifest in the hearts of those who seek it. Through meditative practices, individuals can explore and understand the cosmic past of substances and their spiritual-processual origins before they condensed into lifeless matter (Paradise of Eden). By harnessing willpower and spiritual techniques, these substances can be elevated to support the evolution of human consciousness and redeem the Earth by transforming them into their destined spiritual state (Heavenly Jerusalem). Practical applications of this concept are evident in homeopathy, anthroposophic medicine, and biodynamic agriculture.

The act of Christ on Golgotha fundamentally altered the physical constitution of the Earth as Christ united Himself with it. Since then, human consciousness has evolved to allow the 'spiritual eyes' of the mind and the 'spiritual ears' of the heart to perceive gold in lead and hear the cosmic music of the planets within the metals, thus perceiving and hearing the world in God.

Just as a saint perceives the potential for sanctity in a sinner, so does the alchemist-sage see in lead the potential for metallic sanctity—gold—and in the sanctity of a purified human heart, the presence of Christ within our solar Higher Self. This vision is 'operative,' transforming both the practitioner and the Earth.

The Rosicrucian alchemist does not seek to make physical gold; rather, the true purpose of his work is to intimately unite his soul with that of the metals. By connecting with their spiritual essence, he processes them—and his own consciousness—so that they may express their future divine potential. This journey can culminate in the unity of the soul with the Macrocosmic Christ and ultimately, the Holy Trinity, thereby transforming the Earth into a New Sun, the Heavenly Jerusalem as foretold in the Revelation of St. John.

The Rosicrucian alchemist actualizes the Word of Christ to the letter, proclaiming to all creatures, 'The stone is the Resurrection Body of Christ, the Earth has become the body of Christ, and the human body can become the 'Word' (Logos) of a new creation.' Through his vision of gold as the purest representation of the Holy Trinity within earthly substances, the alchemist seeks to transmute every 'imperfect metal,' first in thought and then within his soul and nature.

The role of the Rosicrucian alchemist is twofold: Firstly, he aids Nature, now shrouded in the darkness of materialism, and suffocated by human decadence, to breathe the presence of God, continuing the deeds of Christ and renewing the spiritual essence of the Universe once again. Secondly, he 'awakens' natural substances—minerals, metals, and even gold itself—to their true nature by liberating their spirits in the creation of remedies and 'elixirs' used to heal illnesses, strengthen life forces, and purify the soul.

'Drinkable Gold,' a gold awakened to its spiritual quality, reflects this 'immortality medicine.' Metals, plants, and minerals are prepared to harness their spiritual essence for healing and transforming the human constitution into an ever more perfect vessel for the Higher Self.

The Rosicrucian alchemist also celebrates the transformation of bread and wine into the body and blood of Christ, extending this transmutation to all of Nature. This profound work is explored both imaginatively and symbolically in the writings of alchemists and their parables, as detailed in the second chapter of this book, 'The Preparation of the Philosopher's Stone.' For Rosicrucian Alchemy, Nature and the Cosmos are intimately connected, forming a living, transparent, and sacred organism—an immense Anthropos mirroring the lesser. Nature is simultaneously the body of God and of man, filled with life, soul, and the holy breath of God.

For Rosicrucian Alchemy, Nature and the Cosmos are intimately related, forming a living, transparent, and sacred world, a vast Anthropos that mirrors the smaller human form. Nature serves simultaneously as the body of God and of man, infused everywhere with life, soul, and the holy breath of God.

'The Sun's blood made the golden embryo grow in the matrix of the mountains. Spiritual beings within the spheres of the seven planets have engendered the seven metals on Earth and the seven life centers (organs) in the embryos of animals and humans. These centers, extending from the genitals to the head, orbit the sun-heart in humans.

The human body is one of many manifestations of the same structural essence found throughout the world; both the human body and Nature are temples created by the Word (Logos), serving as miniature representations of the macrocosmic forces, the Macro-Anthropos.

Awakened human consciousness can perceive this profound relationship. For instance, the spirit of the seven planets corresponds to the creation of seven physical organs, the seven metals within the Earth, and the seven musical notes. This cosmic music, or 'harmony of the spheres' as Kepler called it, resonates in the vibrations of metals and the music of the individual human soul, evident in the interplay of life processes within the human body. This perception arises once we have developed the 'spirit eye' in our head and the 'spirit ear' in our heart.

Understand that the goal of the Ancients' science, which simultaneously cultivated the sciences and virtues, originates from the invisible, unmoving God, whose Will ignites intelligence. This intelligence reveals the unified soul, which gives rise to distinct natures that generate all compounds. Consequently, true knowledge of anything requires understanding of what is superior to it. The Soul, being superior to Nature, allows us to understand Nature; similarly, intelligence, being higher than the soul, helps us comprehend the soul.

Ultimately, intelligence leads us back to the supreme One God, whose essence is beyond comprehension.

The Rosicrucian alchemist projects cosmogony into the future, aligning cosmic forces with the evolving Earth and humanity. He first dissolves material 'hardenings'—the chemical elements—in his mind, then through alchemical processes transforms them into pure life, soul, and spirit. He meditates on the wisdom, beauty, and strength of Nature and the 'sympathy' that unifies all, culminating in the solar fire of the Spirit rising in his heart to unite with Nature's soul, now the dwelling of the Sun Spirit of Christ.

This fire, through a higher cosmogony, does not perish into matter but transforms it, turning Lead into Gold and the human body into a glorified form. As Henry Corbin stated, Alchemy operates as a 'physics of resurrection.' Thus, Rosicrucian alchemy exalts human Nature as Christ's Nature, transforming Soul, Life, and body through the spirit imbued with Christ.

Human organisms and nature are initially governed by a logic of conflict, dominated by dual forces such as will and intellect, action and reflection, substance and form, life and death, inflammation, and sclerosis. This perpetual struggle is symbolized by the two serpents of the Caduceus.

In Rosicrucian alchemy, the work involves meditation and operation, aiming to transform this conflict into love, so that death—seen in Christ—becomes a gateway to a glorious rebirth in the Holy Spirit.

Nature operates in a universe of forms through a rhythmic cycle of 'coagulations' and 'dissolutions,' impressing form upon matter and dissolving it to assume new forms. This cycle of alternation, evolution, and involution—birth, life, death, rebirth—is encapsulated in the alchemical maxim 'solve et coagula.' Nature manifests through continually interacting tensions that neutralize and destroy each other, only to emerge anew. This eternal battle mirrors the alchemical view of nature's transformations and human interactions, akin to the polarizations found in yin and yang, sun and moon, or male and female energies, described as 'Sulphur' and 'Salt.'

Sulphur, Phosphorus, or Carbon, with their fiery and airy nature, and limestone, clay, and silica, embodying water and earth, represent these dynamic forces. This polarity is mirrored in the human body through the interplay between the nervous-sense activity, which underpins our cognitive and sensory perceptions, and the metabolic-limb system, which channels our will and actions. These two forces create a field of force in the 'intermediate world,' aligning closely with the divine manifestations of pure action (solve) and form (coagula), embodied in the cosmic dance of Shakti and Shiva, or the dual aspects of the Sun God: Dionysus and Apollo.

In this dynamic, 'Sulphur'—active and essential—symbolizes the masculine spirit, while 'Salt' aligns more with the passive, feminine soul. The dominance of 'Salt' over 'Sulphur' can lead to sclerosis, while 'Sulphur's' dominance over 'Salt' can result in inflammation. 'Mercury,' serving as a mediator, balances these forces, much like our emotions bridge cognition and action, ensuring health, longevity, and harmony of the soul.

Through its most exalted manifestation as Gold, Mercury symbolizes the rhythm, balance, and harmony of breathing and circulation, essential for spiritual, psychological, and physical health, and embodies unity with Christ. Gold, thus, becomes the 'Water of Life,' transcending even death.

To the 'fallen' man, Nature appears merely as an immense battlefield littered with endless 'corpses,' precipitated by the continual clash of the cosmos's two great forces: the male and female principles of creation.

'Mercury,' the Hermaphrodite, serves as a mediator that unites these opposing forces, heals their divisions, and overcomes imbalance by rhythmically balancing them. In human nature, the Gold/Sun and Silver/Moon process manifest in the rhythms of our physiological functions—breathing (inhalation and exhalation), circulation (systole and diastole), and the cycles of sleeping and waking, fasting, and feasting.

The 'Mercury' process in the body represents rhythms that mediate between the static 'coagulating' tendencies of our Nerve-Sense System (Moon) and the dynamic 'dissolving' tendencies of our Metabolic-Limb System (Sun). These processes are foundational to life: Inhalation and systole contribute to earthly birth (Moon), while exhalation and diastole guide us toward earthly death and rebirth in the spiritual realm (Sun).

Every metal embodies 'Mercury,' which serves to balance the youthful, inflammatory nature of 'Sulphur' and the aging, sclerotic nature of 'Salt.' These opposing forces must be harmonized to maintain health and foster spiritual development. Metals associated with the inner planets—Silver (Moon), Mercury (Mercury), and Copper (Venus)—are in polarity with those of the outer planets—Lead (Saturn), Tin (Jupiter), and Iron (Mars). The ultimate balance of these polarities is represented by Gold (Sun) and mirrors the balance within the human heart between breathing and circulation, the sanctuary of our inner Sun.

Rosicrucian alchemy, understood as a 'science of balance' and an 'art of marriage,' harnesses the 'cosmic sexuality' of 'Sulphur' and 'Salt,' along with the planetary energies of Saturn, Jupiter, Mars, Moon, Mercury, and Venus. These energies are neutralized and elevated in the alchemical creation of our inner solar system's Sun. The alchemist initiates this process by dissolving the imperfect physical states of metals, transforming them into manifestations of life, soul, and spirit—such as through homeopathic potentiation.

Subsequently, the alchemist unites opposing metals and their planetary forces, cultivating the gold of the soul and transmuting the physical body. By marrying the metals of the inner and outer planets, the alchemist reinforces the inner Sun, advancing the creation of a glorified body.

In this schema, Silver acts as the 'Salt' of Mercury, Copper as its 'Sulphur,' while Lead and Iron serve as the 'Salt' and 'Sulphur' of Tin, respectively. This union, when Lead joins with Silver, Tin with Mercury, and Iron with Copper, engenders metaphysical Gold, fostering the soul's spiritual awakening, eternal life, and moral integrity.

This process, ultimately forging a profound bond between humanity and Christ, involves uniting Saturn with the Moon, Jupiter with Mercury, and Mars with Venus, catalyzing the inner Sun. This alchemical wedding—'philosophical incest'—culminates in the union of 'Sulphur' (Sun) and 'Salt' (Moon) within humanity, through which Christ's spirit purifies the soul, revives life, and achieves resurrection. 'Christ is the true Mercurius,' embodying the core principle of Rosicrucian alchemy.

The Chymical Wedding symbolizes the ceremonial union of the 'Red King' (Gold/Sun) with the 'White Queen' (Silver/Moon), as depicted in the 'Parabola'. The King, adorned in gold and purple, holds a rose, while the Queen, crowned in silver, clasps a white lily. This Rosicrucian alchemical process is fundamentally about 'flesh-making'—it seeks not to escape the world but to illuminate it, embodying a 'royal' endeavor that demands 'fidelity to the earth.'

In the detailed symbolism of the 'Parabola' (referenced in the Second Chapter), the vessel for this transformative work is kept 'hermetically sealed' to prevent the 'angel'—the subtle essence of the compound— from escaping, ensuring it condenses and transforms repeatedly. Jacob Böhme likens the residing spiritual body within the visible body to 'oil,' which must be ignited to foster a 'life of joy exalted by everything.

Rosicrucian alchemy heralds a call to heroic virility, challenging the alchemist to transform the 'poison of life' into an elixir of longevity. He is portrayed as a 'solar hero,' a master of the serpentine kundalini energies and a master of mother nature. He binds the hands of the virgin, he transforms torrential waters into the vivifying stone, he subordinates nature which delights in itself to nature which is capable to surpass itself.

Through advancing cosmogony, the alchemist imbues cosmic sexuality with the grace of liberating love—nurturing love between men and women towards their mutual perfection, between craftsmen and their creations, and between kings and queens and their realms.

This dynamic involves the merging of masculine and feminine energies.

The cosmic dance involves the Sun's energy being cast onto Venus, transforming it into Mars, which redirects its vigorous essence towards sacred combat. Subsequently, Mars conditions Mercury to reveal Jupiter, the arbiter of peace, enabling the spirit to weave through the vegetative dream and reshape the global nightmare into a divine vision. Through Jupiter, the Sun's essence reaches the foundational forces of water, moon, and sexuality, reviving fertility to propagate life itself. Ultimately, a reborn Saturn heralds the Golden Age, where Lead transmutes into Gold, allowing the alchemist's consciousness to permeate the mineral realm deeply.

Thus, the secret lies within chalk, the potent limestone, the incorruptible vessel that triumphs over death, and conquers deprivation—the absence of God.

Henceforth, the silent presence of the Rosicrucian alchemist serves as a benediction to all beings. As the secret King, he is the central force that harmonizes heaven and Earth, ensuring cosmic order. Symbolically dead to himself and thus an inexhaustible source of nourishment, he embodies the mystery of 'multiplication' and abundance. Known as the 'panacea,' the elixir of life, or 'drinkable gold,' Christ manifests through the initiated Rosicrucian Alchemist, the 'Knight of the Golden Stone.'

From the 'Philosopher's Stone,' also known as the 'Christ Stone,' flows a red (Sun) and white (Moon) tincture that soothes both soul and body. This Stone is likened to a phoenix, from whose ashes arises a multitude of golden birds, symbolizing the transition from death to resurrection.

Rosicrucian alchemy harnesses the soul's yearning for a dream, not to exploit but to expand it to the universe's magnitude, liberating the soul through love for the world's beauty. When dreams transcend the confines of the individual soul to merge with the world soul, revealing the pristine nature of virgin Nature, the spiritual awakening of Gold ensues. The Stone proclaims: 'I am,' the Divine Name, asking, 'Who dreams?'

This alchemical journey also explores the union of dualities, as portrayed in a fifteenth-century manuscript detailed by Jung in Psychology and Alchemy. In the process of 'mortification'—a prelude to mystical union—the Tree of Life sprouts from both the man's belly and the woman's head, suggesting that each must integrate their opposite traits: men embracing their inner femininity and women their inner masculinity to achieve genuine union.

Therefore, the 'diamond body' in alchemy mirrors the Resurrection body of Christ, symbolized by the 'philosopher's stone'—a diamond-like essence that transcends death and embodies eternal life.

Christian Rosenkreuz, the legendary founder of the Rosicrucian Order, is a pivotal figure in Western Christian esotericism and alchemy. Rudolf Steiner, the founder of anthroposophy, conducted spiritual research suggesting that Christian Rosenkreuz has reincarnated approximately every 100 years since his initial emergence in the 14th century. His profound influence extends into Rosicrucian-inspired Freemasonry and has spurred the creation of key contemporary spiritual movements, including the Theosophical Society, The Golden Dawn, and the Anthroposophic Society, which Steiner himself founded.

The mission of Rosenkreuz and his disciples focuses on advancing Christian spiritual development, aiming to usher individuals into heightened states of spiritual consciousness and physical transformation—elements expected to become more prevalent in the future. His teachings promote the development of individual freedom, selfless love, and mastery of life. Notably, in one of his recent incarnations, Rosenkreuz introduced the I.A.O. mantric meditation, a practice designed to transform physical organization and foster spiritual advancement.

The I.A.O. mantra, standing for 'I am the Alpha and the Omega,' represents the esoteric name of Christ, the Logos and creator of the world. This mantra symbolizes the ultimate goal of humanity's development: the cultivation of individual freedom and selfless love. Rudolf Steiner introduced I.A.O. as a focal point for meditation within his esoteric school, the Christian Community's priest circle. This practice includes foundation stone meditation and eurythmy exercises designed to harmonize thought, emotion, and will.

Various interpretations of the I.A.O. mantra reveal its depth, explored throughout this book, including its role in alchemical processes like the symbolic union of Ignis (Fire – representing willpower and passion) and Aqua (Water – representing dispassionate wisdom). This union is visually represented by a hexagram, composed of intertwining triangles surrounded by the Ouroboros, symbolizing the eternal cycle of birth, death, and rebirth.

Additionally, meditation on the mantras "IehOvA" and the "I.A.O." facilitate a profound connection with the **JehOvA** Moon and the Christ Sun, enhancing the purification, strengthening, and harmonization of mind, body, and spirit. The Rosicrucian Sun and Moon Meditation, introduced at the book's conclusion, combines focusing on merging the Moon and the Sun and mantras **"IehOvA"** and **"I.A.O."** in the heart, and specific breathing techniques to foster this spiritual connection.

In the Rosicrucian context, the I.A.O. mantra also points to Christ's cosmic roles: as the creator, redeemer, and the Lord of Karma. This mantra helps align us with Christ's transformative energy, promoting the evolution of humanity.

This practice not only enlightens and energizes but also helps balance and integrate our cognitive, emotional, and physical functions.

Regular practice of the Sun and Moon Meditation can be a pivotal tool in developing the gifts of freedom, love, and mastery of life that Christ bestows for personal and communal growth. This meditation, along with contemplative goal exploration, empathetic listening, and the contemplative study of Steiner's and Rosenkreuz's teachings, provides a comprehensive approach to spiritual and holistic living.

Thus, developing selfless love through Christ lays the foundation for new, open spiritual communities aimed at furthering humanity's spiritual evolution. It is hoped that engaging in the Sun and Moon Meditation and in those practices will not only advance our personal growth but also contribute to the broader spiritual and social development, connecting us more deeply with Christ, Rudolf Steiner, and Christian Rosenkreuz.

I. Christ, Christian Rosenkreuz, and Rudolf Steiner

Christ

Christ, as referred to here, transcends any specific religious denomination or confession. Since His birth, life on Earth, death, and resurrection, Christ has manifested within the Earth and within us as the embodiment of selfless love. By consciously and purposefully connecting with our higher Self—the Christ consciousness within us—we allow Christ's beneficial influence to reach the innermost parts of our being. Christ is known as the 'I am that I am' from His appearance to Moses in the burning bush, the 'Not I, but Christ in me' from St. Paul's description, and the 'I am the Alpha and Omega' as described in the Revelation of St. John. Inviting Christ to reside and work within us through daily symbol and mantra meditation can, over time, enlighten our thinking, fill our feeling with selfless love, and empower our will to act in alignment with the goals of human evolution.

Christian Rosenkreuz (1378–1484)

Christian Rosenkreuz is the legendary founder of Rosicrucian initiation and the global esoteric brotherhood known as the Rosicrucians. Rudolf Steiner regarded him as one of the highest Christian initiates and spiritual masters, instrumental in guiding humanity towards an understanding of the Christ impulse and the cultivation of Christ consciousness. As a pivotal leader in humanity's spiritual evolution, Rosenkreuz imparts profound 'heart knowledge.' He authored seminal works such as the Temple Legend, the Fama Fraternitatis (1614), and the Confessio Fraternitatis (1615), and inspired Johannes Valentinus Andreae to write the Chymical Wedding of Christian Rosenkreuz

Rudolf Steiner (1861–1925)

Rudolf Steiner was a spiritual scientist and teacher initiated by Christian Rosenkreuz. He revitalized the Rosicrucian teachings, adapting them to suit contemporary human consciousness. Steiner's extensive background in philosophy and science, coupled with his advanced clairvoyant abilities, enabled him to create a practical esoteric training pathway. This pathway not only revitalizes various professional fields but also assists individuals in discovering their personal developmental journeys.

Central to Steiner's philosophy is his personal connection with Christ and Christ consciousness, which fosters community building founded on the principles of freedom, selfless love, and mastery of life.

The Philosopher's Stone

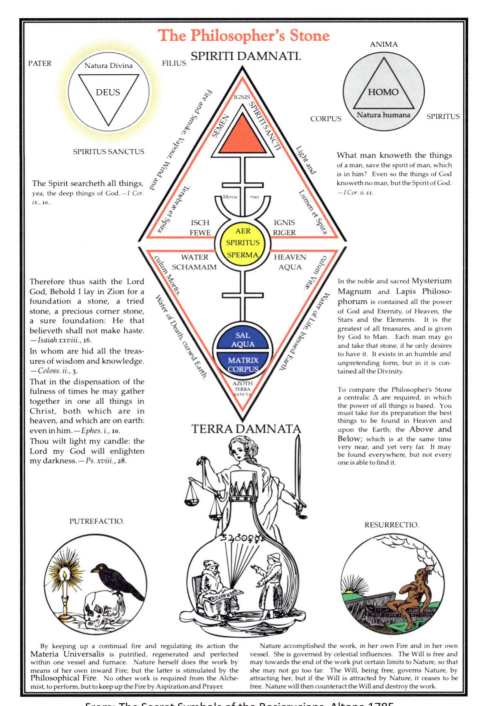

SPIRITI DAMNATI.

PATER — Natura Divina — FILIUS
DEUS
SPIRITUS SANCTUS

ANIMA
HOMO
Natura humana
CORPUS — SPIRITUS

IGNIS
SPIRITUS SANCTI
SEMEN
Fire and Smoke, Vapour, Wind and
Tempest et Spiritus
Light and
Lumen et Spira
Mercurius

ISCH FEWE
AER SPIRITUS SPERMA
IGNIS RIGER
WATER SCHAMAIM
HEAVEN AQUA

culum Vitæ
Water of Life, blessed Earth.
culum Mortis.
Water of Death, cursed Earth.

SAL AQUA
MATRIX CORPUS
AZOTH TERRA SANCTA

TERRA DAMNATA

The Spirit searcheth all things, yea, the deep things of God. —*1 Cor. ix., 10..*

Therefore thus saith the Lord God, Behold I lay in Zion for a foundation a stone, a tried stone, a precious corner stone, a sure foundation: He that believeth shall not make haste. —*Isaiah xxviii.,* 16.

In whom are hid all the treasures of wisdom and knowledge. —*Coloss. ii.,* 3.

That in the dispensation of the fulness of times he may gather together in one all things in Christ, both which are in heaven, and which are on earth: even in him. —*Ephes. i.,* 10.

Thou wilt light my candle: the Lord my God will enlighten my darkness. —*Ps. xviii.,* 28.

What man knoweth the things of a man, save the spirit of man, which is in him? Even so the things of God knoweth no man, but the Spirit of God. —*1 Cor. ii.* 11.

In the noble and sacred Mysterium Magnum and Lapis Philosophorum is contained all the power of God and Eternity, of Heaven, the Stars and the Elements. It is the greatest of all treasures, and is given by God to Man. Each man may go and take that stone, if he only desires to have it. It exists in an humble and unpretending form, but in it is contained all the Divinity.

To compare the Philosopher's Stone a centralic Δ are required, in which the power of all things is based. You must take for its preparation the best things to be found in Heaven and upon the Earth; the Above and Below; which is at the same time very near, and yet very far. It may be found everywhere, but not every one is able to find it.

PUTREFACTIO.

RESURRECTIO.

By keeping up a continual fire and regulating its action the Materia Universalis is putrified, regenerated and perfected within one vessel and furnace. Nature herself does the work by means of her own inward Fire; but the latter is stimulated by the Philosophical Fire. No other work is required from the Alchemist, to perform, but to keep up the Fire by Aspiration and Prayer.

Nature accomplished the work, in her own Fire and in her own vessel. She is governed by celestial influences. The Will is free and may towards the end of the work put certain limits to Nature, so that she may not go too far. The Will, being free, governs Nature, by attracting her, but if the Will is attracted by Nature, it ceases to be free. Nature will then counteract the Will and destroy the work.

From: The Secret Symbols of the Rosicrucians. Altona 1785.

II. The Preparation of the Philosopher's Stone

The fourth stage of Rosicrucian training involves the gradual development of the 'Preparation of the Philosopher's Stone.' This process transforms the physical-spiritual body into the 'Phantom,' which is akin to Christ's resurrection body—a future stage of human development that can already be initiated through esoteric training and initiation.

During this stage, specific mantras are used in conjunction with regulated breathing focused on the heart and lungs. This practice aims to purify the red, oxygen-rich blood of vices and lower desires, and to revitalize the forces in the blue, carbon dioxide-rich blood, turning it into a source of life. In the future, it is posited that the human organism will develop an organ within the heart similar to the green leaves of plants. This organ will convert carbon dioxide (CO_2) into oxygen (O_2) and use carbon (C) to build a future physical form, referred to as the 'Diamond body.' This term reflects the body's transformation into a clear, diamond-like carbon structure, symbolizing the purified and spiritual physical human body of the future.

The preparation of the Philosopher's Stone is a spiritual-physical process carried out during breathing meditation. The spiritual forces of the creative word (mantra) are amplified through regulated breathing to counteract the resistance of the physical body, which is influenced by material forces. This process aids in spiritualizing the physical organization.

As a result, this enhanced mantric breathing meditation enables the human "I" to begin transforming the astral, etheric, and physical bodies into Spirit Self (Manas), Life Spirit (Budhi), and Spirit Man

(Atma), infusing these subtle bodies with wisdom, love, and power. The meditative practices involve the purification of the 'tree of knowledge' (represented by the red, oxygen-rich blood) from vices and desires, and the transformation of the 'tree of death' (represented by the blue, carbon-dioxide-rich blood) into the 'tree of life.'

These transformative practices are foundational in developing the 'three seeds' of wisdom, love, and power, uniting the tree of knowledge and the tree of life within the initiate. This unity lays the groundwork for becoming a citizen of both the physical and spiritual worlds, making personal death seem like a seamless transition for the initiate. They experience the spiritual realm, typically only accessible after death, during their lifetime.

The creation of the Philosopher's Stone may be accelerated by resonance breathing, which involves rhythmic slow and deep breathing at a rate of 5-6 cycles per minute, with circular breathing eliminating the pauses between inhalation and exhalation. This technique allows the spiritual forces active before birth to merge with those experienced after death.

Rosicrucian initiates who create the Philosopher's Stone merge their physical-spiritual body with the multiplied resurrection body of Christ, allowing continuous self-awareness and full awareness of the spiritual surroundings after death—contrasting with the dimmed awareness experienced by non-initiates.

This advanced stage of spiritual-physical development, anticipated for humanity in the distant future, is meticulously prepared by Rosicrucian initiates as a service to humanity.

In Rosicrucian esoteric practice, the stage of Preparing the Philosopher's Stone is achieved through specialized breathing exercises. Humans naturally depend on plants for oxygen, which is crucial for life; plants absorb the carbon dioxide we exhale and release oxygen, creating a sustainable cycle essential for both parties. This interdependence highlights how plants convert carbon into life-sustaining structures, as seen in coal, which is formed from ancient plant remains.

Rosicrucian training builds on this concept by guiding practitioners in controlled breathing exercises aimed at developing an internal mechanism within the human body to transform carbon dioxide back into oxygen, potentially leading to self-sufficiency similar to that of plants. This initiative, still in its nascent stages through esoteric practices, envisions a future where humans might develop plant-like capabilities for self-sustenance.

Through these controlled breathing practices, an individual can internally retain carbon to help build and sustain their physical body, transitioning towards more plant-like characteristics. This state, referred to as aligning with the 'holy love lance,' is typically accessible only to initiates who have reached higher levels of consciousness.

This transformation, which involves the transmutation of human substance based on carbon, embodies the preparation of the 'Philosopher's Stone.' Carbon is the symbol for this alchemical process, but the true Philosopher's Stone emerges only when an individual can create it through disciplined breathing techniques. This sacred knowledge is deeply confidential, passed directly from master to student. Only those who have undergone thorough purification and preparation can receive this wisdom. Public disclosure of these teachings risks misuse by those driven by selfish motives.

Cagliostro and the Philosopher's Stone

According to Rudolf Steiner, Cagliostro was deeply invested in understanding and producing the Philosopher's Stone, along with unraveling the secrets of the mystical pentagram. While often dismissed as fanciful or symbolic, Cagliostro insisted these subjects were based on factual truths. He claimed that the Philosopher's Stone could dramatically extend human life, possibly up to 5,527 years, and suggested that through specific training, one could live indefinitely beyond the physical body.

He clarified, however, that mastering these arts doesn't make one immune to physical death, like from unexpected accidents, unless the adept allows it. Rather than avoiding death entirely, he spoke of a different understanding of death. For those who master the Philosopher's Stone, physical death is just a superficial event. While it might seem like a significant endpoint for most, for the adept, it's merely an event observed by others. In essence, these masters have learned to live independently of their physical body, experiencing during their lifetime what typically happens at death.

This perspective implies that the consciousness of an adept can essentially outlive their physical body, and become already during life citizens of both worlds, the earthly and the spiritual word. This spiritual world is only experienced by the uninitiated in a more or less dimmed down way after death. The initiated who has developed the Philosopher's Stone is fully aware of both, the physical and the spiritual world, can perceive and act in both and can build a bridge his experiences in both worlds.

The use of the Philosopher's Stone was available for may human beings during the Atlantean epoch. Current overestimations of medical advancements could stem from subconscious memories of past lives, suggesting that what we consider modern medical breakthroughs might actually be rediscoveries of ancient knowledge. Spiritual Science aims to prepare humanity for such profound insights, reminiscent of a time during the Atlantean Epoch when knowledge and skills of transcending death was more common.

The Breathing Process in Occult Development

When meditating regularly, exercises for intuition can influence more than just the etheric body; they also impact the supersensible forces within the physical body. However, these changes aren't visible through normal sensory observation and can only be recognized by those with clairvoyant abilities. This transformation comes from a deeper consciousness that has moved beyond past experiences, both internal and external.

Intuitive experiences are subtle and nuanced, especially when contrasted with the physical body, which can seem relatively crude at its current stage of evolution. The physical body often poses significant challenges to practicing intuition effectively. Despite these hurdles, with enough dedication, energy, and calmness, these challenges can be overcome. As one progresses, involuntary physical actions, like breathing, may come under conscious control to better harmonize the body with internal spiritual practices.

Ideally, developing intuition should happen through consciousness exercises alone, without involving the physical body. But due to the substantial barriers the physical body presents, some initial physical exercises might be necessary. These should be carried out under the guidance of an experienced teacher to avoid risks.

One such practice involves specific, time-limited breathing exercises that correspond to certain psycho-spiritual laws. Breathing, a physical act, when performed in this regulated manner, embodies a psycho-spiritual law, imprinting spirituality directly onto physical existence and transforming the physical matter itself.

This leads to the 'transmutation of the physical body', which is the 'working with the Philosopher's Stone'. Every true intuition can be considered a working with the philosopher's stone because it invokes the powers that bridge the supersensible world with the sensory world.

The fourth stage of Rosicrucian training focuses on creating the Philosopher's Stone, a concept deeply veiled in secrecy. By the late 18th century, public references to this esoteric idea began to emerge. For example, a remark in a central German newspaper subtly acknowledged its existence, stating: "The Philosopher's Stone is real, and it remains unknown only to a few. Many have unknowingly possessed it." This statement, while literal, demands profound understanding and is not just metaphorical.

Rosicrucians approach reality in ways that go beyond simple moral improvement, delving into deep physiological changes affecting both the Earth and humanity. Consider human respiration, which is fundamental to esoteric development. Normally, we breathe in oxygen that combines with our body's carbon to form carbon dioxide, which we then exhale. Without regulation, this process could dangerously increase atmospheric carbon dioxide levels, threatening our survival. Plants are essential in this cycle, absorbing carbon dioxide, using the carbon, and releasing oxygen, thus maintaining ecological balance.

Future advancements might enable humans to perform what plants do now, particularly carbon sequestration, through evolved respiratory and cardiovascular processes. Esoteric teachings propose that through controlled breathing, humans will not release carbon dioxide but instead transform it into carbon, enhancing their physical structure independently.

This vision aligns with the mythology of the Holy Grail. Through precise breathing techniques, humans could internally produce carbon in forms like graphite or diamond, mirroring the pure essence of plants. This process of creating a translucent, yet softer form of diamond within the body is known as the 'Preparation of the Philosopher's Stone.'

The sensitive nature of such knowledge has historically required secrecy. A materialistic perspective might see this as an opportunity for profitable exploitation, highlighting why such profound insights must remain protected. These secrets should only be disclosed when humanity has achieved a certain level of moral and intellectual maturity, beyond selfish thinking.

Humans possess lungs, organs that fill with air when we inhale and empty upon exhalation, drawing air into their finest branches. However, it's not just air we breathe; the spirit also permeates the air around us. When we inhale, we take in this spirit, and when we exhale, we release some of the absorbed spirit back into the world. This rhythmic, spirit-infused breathing fosters both personal spiritual growth and enriches the external spiritual environment.

The spirit imparted into each exhaled breath is profoundly significant, cultivated through our thoughts. Each thought expelled with our breath shapes and spreads our spiritual essence.

Inhalation links us to our inner self and our past, intertwining with our memories and the demands of our karma. This act of breathing in reinforces our self-awareness, reminding us of our moral duties and intentions set before birth to better ourselves. This inward breath reflects the contracting nature of autumn and winter.

In contrast, exhalation is an act of giving and connecting with the world, associated with the future and freedom. This outward breath promotes liberation and selflessness as we share our essence, deepening our bond to our destiny and the future we aim to create, reminiscent of our ancient connections with higher spiritual beings. This release occurs nightly as we sleep and mirrors the expansive rhythms of spring and summer.

Breathing is intrinsically linked to the Word, aiming to transform our blood—our 'I'—just as the Holy Spirit is connected to Christ's healing wisdom. This transformation resembles the formation of the New Jerusalem, a spiritual realm we are called to co-create. Each breath is a step toward this divine creation.

Individuals seeking personal growth should start by progressively mastering control over their inner forces, beginning with their breathing. This control is achieved by consciously regulating inhalation and exhalation. During inhalation, the forces of the 'I' are activated, linking individuals to cosmic powers that emanate from the heart. On the other hand, during exhalation and when holding the breath, these 'I' forces retreat inward towards the heart, helping to create a solid internal center.

Through such practices, students realize that by deliberately performing these breathing exercises, they can gradually gain mastery over their 'I' forces. However, it's essential to emphasize that these exercises should not be undertaken without proper instruction. No one should start these practices alone without first receiving specific guidance from a knowledgeable teacher.

In the pursuit of inner development, it is essential that each part of the human body be gradually spiritualized, significantly influenced by what is termed the divine breath. This spiritualization begins with the breath, known as 'Odem,' which is so central to the process that the transformed spiritual body is referred to as 'atma' or 'atman.' This term is the root of the German word for breath, 'atem.' Reflecting teachings from the Old Testament, humans are said to have received the breath of life at the beginning of their earthly existence, aligning with ancient wisdom that views the breath of life as something that must be continually spiritualized, considering atman as the ultimate divine manifestation of the breath.

However, the process of spiritualization extends beyond the breath. To fully spiritualize the entire body, not only the breath but also the blood—the physical manifestation of the 'I' that is continually renewed by the breath—must be infused with a strong spiritual impulse. Christianity deepens this concept through the mystery of blood and the internal fire within humans.

Practicing exercises for spiritual development, such as conscious breathing, affects not just the etheric body but also reaches the supersensible forces of the physical body. Through these practices, individuals can activate the forces of their 'I,' connecting them with universal energies that emanate from the heart during inhalation and help establish a solid inner center during exhalation. As practitioners consciously engage in these breathing exercises, they progressively master the forces of their 'I.'

It is critical, however, that such practices are not attempted alone without proper instruction, due to the profound transformations involved that require expert guidance.

This evolution within the human body is analogous to the role of plants: just as plants absorb carbon dioxide and release oxygen, supporting life, humans will eventually internalize this process. Through further development and transformation of heart and respiratory functions, humans will take over this plant process and consciously manage it internally. This rhythmic breathing not only spiritualizes the breath but also the blood, leading to a comprehensive spiritualization of the being.

Moreover, the esoteric connection between internal human processes and external cosmic events is profound. Just as lightning and thunder interact in the cosmos, the fire within our blood and the activity within our nervous system generate thoughts, similar to internal thunder. This parallels cosmic thunder and lightning, showing that human thoughts are a microcosmic reflection of macrocosmic events.

Ultimately, by understanding and integrating these teachings, individuals learn to recognize the interconnectedness of all life and existence, seeing the divine spark within as a reflection of the vast, unfolding universe outside. This comprehensive spiritual science reveals deep truths about human evolution and our potential to transcend ordinary physical existence by spiritualizing our most fundamental processes.

The Coherence Breathing

Resonant Frequency Breathing involves breathing evenly through the nose, inhaling, and exhaling deeply at a slow pace, with each phase lasting 5 – 6 seconds. This technique employs circular breathing, meaning there is no pause between inhalation and exhalation, filling the lungs completely from the bottom up, starting at the diaphragm.

The practice of Resonant Frequency Breathing synchronizes breathing rhythms with heart rate variability and blood pressure rhythm. This synchronization creates a resonance effect, amplifying heart rate variability, indicating that the body is becoming more flexible, adaptable, and balanced. This breathing technique enhances the coordination and balance between the Nerve Sense System (responsible for perceiving, thinking, and imagining) and the Metabolic Limb System (involved in digestion, movement, and action), as well as between periods of strain and recovery. Consequently, the Rhythmic System, which includes breathing and circulation, is strengthened.

Additionally, this breathing technique significantly improves emotion regulation, increasing awareness of emotional states and transforming negative emotions such as fear, anxiety, anger, and despair into positive feelings like love, compassion, courage, and enthusiasm. During this slow and deep breathing process, the heart and brain achieve a state of coherence, characterized by synchronized high-amplitude electrical activity. This physiological state is similar to the effects experienced during positive emotional states, states of flow, or deep engagement.

The Sun and Moon Meditation, described at the end of this book, incorporates coherence or resonant frequency training, combining paced breathing with visualization, mantra meditation, and the cultivation of positive feelings and intentions. Coherence Breathing specifically aligns the activity of the brain, heart, and pelvic organs, enhancing the transformative impact of the Moon and Sun imagination and the mantras **"IehOvA"** and **"I.A.O."** on the physical body. This can help overcome conditioned abnormal physiological patterns, learned responses, and inherited characteristics.

Furthermore, Coherence Breathing focuses and centralizes consciousness in the heart, bridging breathing and circulation. This centralization allows the spiritual power of the mantras to transform the heart and blood, impacting the entire physical organization. By balancing inhalation and exhalation and removing pauses, circular breathing connects past experiences (inhalation) with future possibilities (exhalation). This practice fosters undivided attention and a present mindedness that intuitively perceives the spirit of Self, others, and nature.

'Jachim' and 'Boaz' and the 'Golden Legend'

Jachin and Boaz are the names of two pillars at the entrance of Solomon's Temple, built under the guidance of King Solomon and King Hiram Abiff's builders. These pillars symbolize the cycles of birth and death:

Jachin, often called the Pillar of Birth, represents the point where consciousness enters the sensory world, similar to the sunrise moving through the zodiacal constellations. It marks the shift from the night to the day side of the cosmos. Esoterically, Jachin is seen as the celestial gateway to life's daytime phase, where the divine essence, once spread across the Macrocosm, begins to manifest within individuals, transforming each person into a microcosm—a miniature universe embodying the internalized divine.

Boaz, the Pillar of Death, symbolizes the portal through which the soul passes back into the spiritual realm upon death. It embodies the concept that personal strengths and inner qualities developed during life are then spread throughout the cosmos. 'Boaz' indicates that qualities once cultivated internally will be found externalized across the universe, where we exist beyond death.

Human life progresses between these pillars, transitioning from Jachin to Boaz, exploring both sensory and spiritual dimensions. In our physical lives, we engage directly with the world around us through touch and interaction. Conversely, between death and rebirth in the spiritual realm, our existence transcends physical constraints, becoming part of the broader cosmic life. This state offers a profound sense of movement and balance that differs from earthly balance, which is restricted by gravity and physical form.

As we navigate from life to death, we evolve from recognizing the divine within ourselves to merging with the universal divine. This passage between Jachin and Boaz underscores a deep, cyclic journey of growth and understanding, reflecting the soul's eternal pursuit of evolution and enlightenment.

Inhalation and Exhalation: The Tree of Knowledge, and the Tree of Life

According to the "Golden Legend," Seth, son of Adam and successor to Abel, was granted a rare privilege upon reaching maturity: a glimpse into Paradise, bypassing the guarding angel with the flaming sword. In this sacred space, Seth witnessed the extraordinary sight of the Tree of Life and the Tree of Knowledge intertwined. From these unified trees, he collected three seeds, which he later placed in Adam's mouth at his father's passing.

A mighty tree sprang from Adam's grave, radiating a glow akin to a fiery blaze to those with psychic senses. Observers noted letters within this glow, "J B," representing the profound declaration, "I am Who was; I am Who is; I am Who will be."

- This tree split into three segments, each pivotal in world evolution:
- One segment became Moses' magical staff.
- Another was used in the construction of Solomon's Temple, housing ancient wisdom.

The final piece, after being submerged in a healing pool aiding the lame and blind, was transformed into the bridge Christ crossed en route to his Crucifixion and eventually into the Cross itself.

This legend holds deep symbolic meanings, particularly in the context of Rosicrucian training concerning the Philosopher's Stone. This stage involves specific treatments of red blood, deemed significant by Goethe as "a very special fluid" and emphasized throughout esoteric traditions. Red blood, vital for its life-sustaining properties, arises from the inhalation of oxygen—a critical process discussed in both the legend and the Bible.

The legend and scriptural texts recount humanity's expulsion from Paradise, transitioning from a higher spiritual existence to a physical form—a significant evolutionary step depicted by the inhalation of life's breath, allowing the creation of red blood. This moment marks the descent from a divine existence within the fluidic pre-life to a corporeal life necessitating oxygen and lungs.

Visually, one can imagine a person outlined by the flow of red blood, representing the Tree of Knowledge. The act of consuming this metaphorical fruit, the red blood, is seen as the original sin leading to expulsion from Paradise to prevent access to the Tree of Life.

Additionally, a concurrent metaphorical tree, filled with blue-red blood—symbolic of death—exists within us. Over time, it is believed that expanded consciousness will transform this tree, turning the symbol of death into a new Tree of Life.

The legend positions Seth as an initiate who could perceive the divine-spiritual intertwinement of these trees. At Adam's death, he placed the seeds from these trees into Adam's mouth, symbolizing the latent divine potential within humanity—manas (mind), buddhi (intellect), and atman (spirit).

This narrative not only reveals the tripartite divine nature inherent from humanity's inception but also guides us through our spiritual evolution. The wood from this metaphysical tree was used not only in sacred artifacts like Moses' staff and the Cross but also symbolizes the journey through initiation, where lower aspects of our being are transcended by higher spiritual realities.

Today, our spiritual journey is reflected in the pillars of Jachin and Boaz, representing the intertwined dualities of life and knowledge, death and rebirth. These pillars challenge us to merge these dual aspects through expanded consciousness into a unified whole, marked by the profound union of the red and blue-red energies within us. This evolutionary leap calls us to realize our full spiritual potential, blending these energies into a harmonious state of being.

The Two Blood Circuits of the Heart

"Blood striving toward the breath in the lungs symbolizes humanity's quest for the cosmos. (Exhalation – The author) Conversely, the breath in the lungs, striving toward the blood in the heart, represents the cosmos embracing humanity. (Inhalation – The author) The journey of blood toward the heart epitomizes the refined process of dying, where the blood, enriched with carbon dioxide, mirrors this delicate transition.

Humanity continuously merges into the cosmos through the bloodstream, a process that becomes pronounced after death as it encompasses the entire physical being through the blood...

The Christ mystery unveils the profound interplay between the heart and the lungs, where the cosmos and humanity are interwoven. This dynamic includes:

The Sun, which guides humanity from the cosmos to Earth.

The Moon, which leads humanity from Earth back into the cosmos.

In broader terms:

The flow from the lungs to the heart reflects the descent of Christ to Earth.

The movement from the heart to the lungs mirrors the ascent of humanity into the spirit world, guided by the Christ impulse after death.

41

Thus, the mystery of Golgotha resides between the heart and the lungs in every human being, manifesting in a deeply physiological sense." Rudolf Steiner.

Dr. Ita Wegman and the Philosopher's Stone

The 'Philosopher's Stone' symbolizes a crucial phase in Rosicrucian spiritual evolution, mirroring significant processes within the human body where carbon is key. On Earth, carbon connects to the 'Philosopher's Stone' and influences it through spiritual forces.

Historically, humans had a more ethereal and flexible physical form that was invisible and luminous. Over time, as humans formed a deeper connection with Earth—described in the Bible as the Fall of Man triggered by Lucifer—our bodies became denser and more visible. This transformation marked humanity's deeper engagement with earthly substances, leading to increased physical density and the introduction of death into human existence. The original, more vital form of the body, known as the phantom, gradually lost its influence, leading to a hardening and decay of the physical form.

Reflecting on a key event in human evolution—the Mystery of Golgotha—it's evident that Christ's sacrifice offered humanity a path to counteract these forces of decay. This intervention was timely as humanity was at a critical low point, with the forces of decay strong and the risk of losing essential human qualities high. The revitalizing forces introduced at Golgotha gave humanity the potential to reverse the densification and restore the body's original flexibility.

This narrative delves into the depths of human evolutionary mysteries, suggesting that the physical body's salvation from densification is closely linked to the creation of the 'Philosopher's Stone.'

The dual nature of human blood—oxygen-rich red blood and carbon dioxide-rich blue blood—plays a pivotal role in our physical and spiritual existence. The transition from a godlike state to earthly beings, as depicted in the Bible when Jehovah breathes life into Adam, involved this critical respiratory process. The red blood, associated with life and earthly engagement, and blue blood, associated with cosmic aspirations, highlight a continuous striving toward the cosmos through our circulatory and respiratory processes.

This ongoing cycle suggests that while inhaling oxygen supports earthly life, exhaling carbon dioxide represents a refined dying process within us. However, this 'death' is also a call to 'Die and Become,' a principle crucial for achieving higher states of being. This concept foresees the transformation of our blue blood into a 'Tree of Life,' symbolizing a significant metamorphosis in human development.

The critical situation of humanity before the Mystery of Golgotha pointed to a potential loss of balance between life forces and physical decay. Christ's manifestation on Earth brought new etheric forces that reconnected humanity with primal life forces, offering a new potential for evolution.

Looking forward, the transformation of 'death' into a new 'Tree of Life' involves transcending earthly drives and refining our red blood. Humans must evolve to utilize carbon dioxide not as a waste product but as a catalyst for higher life, similar to plants that use carbon dioxide harmlessly.

As humanity progresses, this transformative process will likely reduce carbon dioxide emissions, instead retaining and transforming it to enhance life. This change will manifest predominantly in the heart and proceed towards the head, symbolizing a revitalization of our etheric body and potentially restoring our physical form's original agility.

The creation of the 'Philosopher's Stone' involves this profound transformation of the physical and etheric bodies, leading to a luminous and flexible physical form that aligns with the spiritual evolution of humanity. This process is akin to alchemists' work, where human beings are seen as vessels for transformative processes that blend spiritual and physical life processes.

The Rosicrucian allegory of the mystical bridegroom and bride, imprisoned and transformed through the purifying power of the sun, encapsulates the alchemical processes of death, purification, and rebirth, leading to enlightenment and the union of earthly and divine knowledge. This allegory is pivotal for understanding the holistic approach to healing and spiritual evolution, suggesting that transcending our materialistic confines can lead to overall well-being and spiritual enlightenment.

The Chymical Wedding of Christian Rosenkreuz, anno 1459

The Chymical Wedding of Christian Rosenkreuz, published in 1616, attributes its authorship to Johann Valentin Andreae and is traditionally linked with Christian Rosenkreuz. It stands out from the earlier Rosicrucian manifestos, the Fama Fraternitatis and the Confessio Fraternitatis, due to its distinct allegorical style and content. The narrative unfolds over Seven Days of an Alchemistic Journey, describing the union of the purified human soul with the Spirit of Nature (Christ) and delineating the spiritual and alchemical initiation of Christian Rosenkreuz.

The text vividly illustrates a series of processions involving trials, purifications, symbolic death and rebirth, and ascension. It starts with Christian Rosenkreuz receiving an invitation to a Royal Wedding and his initiation as a 'Knight of the Golden Stone' in the year 1459— remarkably, around 150 years prior to its publication. This 'alchemistic wedding' symbolizes the initiation into the spirit of nature, aimed at the complete individualization and spiritualization of the physical body, a gift from both Cosmos and Earth.

Contrastingly, the 'mystical wedding' represents the union of the higher Self within us with the purified soul, differing significantly from the alchemistic path. The narrative of the Chymical Wedding is meant not just for reading but for deep contemplation and meditation, encouraging engagement with the imagery through our thinking, feeling, and will.

Rudolf Steiner's interpretations of the seven days' proceedings offer invaluable insights that aid in preparing the soul for an effective meditation of this profound spiritual content. For further study and meditation, three critical aspects highlighted include:

- The Five Principles of the Knights of the Golden Stone: These principles outline the ethical and spiritual framework guiding the initiates.
- The Encounter with the 'Cruel Lion' (Self-recognition): This represents a pivotal moment of self-awareness and acknowledgment of one's inner challenges.
- The Struggle to Overcome Fear and Commit to Spiritual Development: This aspect focuses on the internal battles that one must endure to progress spiritually.

Each element serves as a stepping stone for deeper understanding and personal growth, making the Chymical Wedding not only a rich literary work but also a guide to spiritual enlightenment and initiation.

The Five Principles of the Knights of the Golden Stone

'In five sentences, it is summarized what guides souls that wish to work in human life in the spirit of Christian Rosenkreuz:

1. They should adhere solely to the spirit manifested in nature's creation, striving to extend natural works through human endeavors.

2.	Their work should not cater to mere human desires but should utilize these desires as conduits for spiritual activities.

3.	They are to serve humanity with love, thereby allowing the active spirit to manifest in interpersonal relationships.

4.	They should remain unaffected by worldly values, focusing instead on the value derived from the spirit inherent in all human labor.

5.	Like prudent alchemists, they must avoid conflating the physical with the spiritual, recognizing that physical means, such as those promising prolonged life, hold value only when revealing the spiritual truths they embody."

The Encounter of the 'Cruel Lion' (Self- Recognition)

"The encounter with the "cruel lion" at the second gate symbolizes the spiritual seeker's journey towards self-recognition. The Brother of the Rosy Cross experiences this moment as an imaginative force acting upon his deeper emotional realms. However, he must yet discern its significance concerning his spiritual standing. Unknown to him, a judgment is rendered by the "Guardian" at the lion's side. Reassuringly, the Guardian, referencing a letter also unknown to the Brother, declares, "Now may God welcome me, the person whom I have long wished to see."

The "cruel lion" emerges as a reflection of the Brother of the Rosy Cross's soul condition, casting a mirror on his own essence within the spiritual world. This reflection is not his human form as understood in the sensory realm but rather an imaginative animal representation. In the sensory world, human drives, affections, feelings, and will impulses are shaped by sensory perceptions and cognitions, all products of the sensory realm. To transcend this, one must become aware of those aspects within themselves that are free from sensory confines, guided onto the correct path by spiritual gifts anew.

This introspective vision is afforded to the Brother of the Rosy Cross during his encounter with the lion, representing his pre-human essence. It's important to clarify that this spiritual perception of one's pre-human form is unrelated to the concept of animality as described by conventional Darwinism. The animal representation belongs solely to the imaginative realm and represents a subconscious aspect of human nature within the sensory world. The notion that part of his essence, constrained by the sensory body, has not yet achieved human form is captured in the mood with which the Brother of the Rosy Cross enters the castle.

The passage explores the journey of spiritual awakening and the obstacles faced by those bound to sensory judgments. It highlights the essential purity of perception required to genuinely engage with the spiritual world, as exemplified by the Brother of the Rosy Cross.

The narrative contrasts those who approach the spiritual realm with a proper soul mood, ready to encounter the "cruel lion" without the distortions of sensory-bound understanding, with those who fail to prepare their inner selves adequately. These unprepared souls, although they physically see the lion, are not deeply affected by the spiritual vision due to their reliance on familiar sensory judgments. Their claims of seeing profound concepts such as Plato's ideas or Democritus's atoms are depicted as empty boasts, revealing their inability to genuinely perceive or connect with the invisible realities of the spiritual world.

The text criticizes this superficial engagement, pointing out the necessity for a true seeker to abandon old modes of judgment and embrace a new, spiritually aligned way of seeing. The Brother of the Rosy Cross, aware of his limitations, does not pretend to possess capabilities he lacks. Instead, he acknowledges his powerlessness, which paradoxically becomes a source of spiritual strength. His admission and the humility to recognize his bounds contrast sharply with the arrogance of others who claim abilities they do not possess.

By the end of the second day, his acceptance of spiritual powerlessness—symbolized by his being literally bound—serves as a transformative experience. This binding is not merely physical but represents his submission to the spiritual lessons of humility and patience. It's suggested that only through enduring these binds, and maintaining awareness in the face of apparent powerlessness, can one's inner weakness be alchemically transmuted into true spiritual strength."

The Struggle to Overcome Fear and Commit to Our Spiritual Development.

In his book, 'The Alchemical Wedding,' Denis Klocek describes the process as follows:

In the allegory, Christ represents the Bridegroom, and the human soul is portrayed as the Bride. Currently, their relationship is akin to an engagement, with the prospect of marriage symbolizing a deep commitment. The Bridegroom, Christ, is ready and eager to unite, but the Bride—the human soul—needs more time to adjust and fully commit to this profound union.

For the true 'wedding'—the full unification of Christ and the soul—to occur, both parties must first reconcile their hopes and needs, reaching a state of mutual readiness and commitment. The soul, in particular, often hesitates, grappling with the daunting prospects of uncertainty, emotional challenges, and the vast unknowns that accompany such a spiritual commitment.

This dynamic of misunderstanding and the discomfort brought on by uncertainty are central themes in Christian Rosenkreuz's journey, as depicted in "The Alchemical Wedding." The subtitle, 'The Initiate of

Misunderstanding,' underscores the recurring challenges of misinterpretation and the profound spiritual growth that arises from navigating these challenges.

AUREUM SECULUM REDIVIVUM

or

The Ancient Golden Age,

which has disappeared from the Earth, but will reappear;

whose germ is beginning to sprout, and will bear blossom and fruit,

by

HENRICUS MADATHANUS THEOSOPHUS,

Medicus & tandem, Dei gratia, aureæ crucis frater.

Translated from the German.

"If there is one among You who is deficient in wisdom, let him pray to the spirit of truth, who comes to the simple-minded, but does not obtrude upon any one, and he will surely obtain it."—*Jacob. Epist. v. 5.*

Symbolum Authoris:

Centrum Mundi: Granum Fundi.

From: The Secret Symbols of the Rosicrucians. Altona, 1785.

The Golden Age Restored, by Henricus Madathanus, ca 1621/22.

"While I was meditating upon the wonders of the Highest and the secrets of hidden Nature and the fiery and fervent love of the neighbor, I recalled the white harvest which Reuben, the son of Leah, had found in the fields and had given the mandrakes Rachel had gotten from Leah for sleeping with the patriarch Jacob. But my thought went much more profound and led me further to Moses, how he had made a potable of the solar calf cast by Aaron, and how he had it burned with fire, ground to powder, strewed it upon the waters, and gave it to the Children of Israel to drink. And I marveled most about this prompt and ingenious destruction God's hand had wrought.

But after pondering over it for some time, my eyes were opened, just as happened with the two disciples at Emmaus who knew the Lord in the Breaking of Bread, and my heart burned within me. But I laid down and began to sleep. And, lo, in my dream, King Solomon appeared to me, in all his might, wealth, and glory, leading beside him all the women of his harem: there were threescore queens, and fourscore concubines, and virgins without number, but one was his gentle dove, most beautiful and dearest to his heart, and according to Catholic custom she held a magnificent procession wherein the Centrum was highly honored and cherished, and its name was like an out-ointment, the fragrance of which surpassed all spices. Its fiery spirit was a key to opening the temple, entering the Holy Place, and grasping the altar's horns.

Solomon showed me the unified Centrum in the trigone center when the procession ended and opened my understanding. I became aware that behind me stood a nude woman with a bloody wound in her breast, out of which came forth blood and water, but the joints of her thighs were like jewels, the work of the hands of a cunning workman, her navel was like a round goblet, which wanted not liquor, her belly was like a heap of wheat set about with roses, her two breasts were like two young roses that are twins, her neck was as a tower of ivory, her eyes like the fish pools in Heshbon by the gate of Bathrabbim; her nose was as the tower of Lebanon which looks towards Damascus. Her head was like Carmel, and the hair of her head was tied in many folds, like the king's purple. But her garments, which she threw off, lay at her feet and were all unsightly, stinking, and poisonous.

And she began to speak: "I have put off my coat; how shall I put it on? I have washed my feet; how shall I defile them? The watchmen that went about the city found me; they smote me, they wounded me and took away my veil from me. Then was I stricken with fear and not conscious and fell upon the ground; but Solomon bade me stand up again and said: be not afraid when thou dost see Nature bare, and the most hidden which is beneath heaven and upon the earth. She is beautiful as Tirzah, comely as Jerusalem, terrible as an army with banners. Still, nevertheless, she is the pure, chaste virgin out of whom Adam was made and created. Sealed and hidden is the entrance to her house, for she dwells in the garden and sleeps in the twofold caves of Abraham on the field Ephron. Her palace is the depths of the Red Sea, and in the deep transparent chasms, the air hath given her birth and the fire hath brought her up, wherefore she is a queen of the country, milk and honey hath she in her breasts. Yea, her lips are like a dripping honeycomb, honey and milk are under her tongue, and the smell of her garments is like the fragrance of Lebanon to the Wise but an abomination to the ignorant." And Solomon said further: "Rouse thee, look upon all my women and see if you can find her equal."

And forthwith, the woman had to cast off her garments, and I looked at her, but my mind had lost the power of judgment, and mine eyes were held so that I did not recognize her.

But as Solomon observed my weakness, he separated his women from this nude woman. He said: "Thy thoughts are vain, and the sun hath burned out thy mind, and thy memory is as black as the fog, so thou canst not judge aright, so if thou wouldst not forfeit thy concern and take advantage of the present opportunity, then can the bloody sweat and snow-white tears of this nude virgin again refresh thee, cleanse thine understanding and memory and restore it fully, so that thine eyes may perceive the wonders of the Highest, the height of the uppermost, and thou shalt really fathom the foundations of all Nature, the power and operation of all the Elements, and thine understanding will be as fine silver, and thy memory as gold, the colors of all precious stones will appear before thine eyes and thou wilt know their production, and thou wilt know how to separate good from evil, the goats from the sheep. Thy life will be very peaceful, but Aaron's cymbals will awaken you from sleep and the harp of David, my father, from thy slumber."

After Solomon thus spoke, I was very much more afraid. I was exceedingly terrified, partly because of his heartbreaking works and partly because of the great glamour and splendor of the present queenly woman. Solomon took me by the hand and led me through a wine cellar into a secret but very stately hall, where he refreshed me with flowers and apples. Still, its windows were made of transparent crystals, and I looked through them. And he said: "What dost thou see?"

I replied: "I can only see from this hall into the hall I just left, and on the left stands thy queenly woman, and on the right the nude virgin, and her eyes are redder than wine, her teeth whiter than milk, but her garments at her feet are more unsightly, blacker, and filthier than the brook of Kidron."

"From all of them, choose one," said Solomon, "to be thy beloved. I esteem her and my queen alike and highly, pleased as I am with the loveliness of my wives, so little do I care about the abomination of her garments."

And as soon as the king had thus spoken, he turned around and conversed amicably with one of his queens. Amongst these was a hundred-year-old stewardess with a grey cloak, a black cap upon her head, bedecked with numberless snow-white pearls and lined with red velvet, and embroidered and sewn artfully with blue and yellow silk, and her cloak was adorned with divers Turkish colors and Indian figures.

This old woman beckoned to me secretly and swore unto me a holy oath that she was the mother of the nude virgin, that she had been born from her body, and that she was a chaste, pure, and secluded virgin, that until now she had not suffered any man to look upon her. Although she had let herself be used everywhere among the many people on the streets, no one had ever seen her naked before now. No one had touched her, for she was the virgin of whom the Prophet said: Behold, we have a son born unto us in secret, who is transformed beside others; behold, the virgin had brought forth, such a virgin as is called Apdorossa, meaning: secretly, she who cannot suffer others. But while this her daughter was unwed, she had her marriage portion lying under her feet because of the present danger of the war so that she would not be robbed of it by some roving soldiery and denuded of her stately treasure.

However, I should not be frightened because of her disgusting garments but choose her daughter before all others for the delight of my love and life. Then she would give and reveal to me a lye to clean her garments. Then, I would obtain a liquid salt and non-combustible oil for my housekeeping and an immeasurable treasure, and her right hand would always caress me. Her left hand would be under my head.

And as I then wanted to declare myself categorically upon this matter, Solomon turned around again, looked upon me, and said: "I am the wisest man on earth, beautiful and pleasing are my wives, and the glamour of my queens surpasses the gold of Ophir; the adornments of my concubines overshadow the rays of the sun, and the beauty of my virgins surpass the rays of the moon, and as heavenly as are my women, my wisdom is unfathomable and my knowledge is inexplicable."

After which I answered and, half afraid, I bowed: "Lo, I have found grace in thine eyes, and since I am poor, give me this nude virgin. I choose her amongst all others for the duration of my life. Though her garments are filthy and torn, I will clean them and love her with all my heart, and she shall be my sister, my bride, because she hath ravished mine heart with one of her eyes, with one chain of her neck."

When I had thus spoken, Solomon gave her unto me, and there was a great commotion in the hall of his women, so that I was awakened by it, and I knew not what had happened to me. Nevertheless, I believed it to be, but a dream and I thought many subtle thoughts about my dream until the morning.

But after I had arisen and said my prayers, Lo! I saw the garments of the nude virgin upon my bed but no trace of her. And I began to be greatly afraid, and all my hair stood upright upon my head, and my whole body was bathed in a cold sweat. Still recalling my dream, I took it to heart and thought about it again in fear of the Lord. But my thoughts did not explain it, so I dared not to scrutinize the garments, much less to recognize anything in them. I then changed my sleeping chamber and left the garments in it for some time out of ignorance, believing that something peculiar would happen to me if I were to touch them or turn them over. Still, in my sleep, the smell of the garments had poisoned me. It inflamed me violently so that my eyes could not see the time of mercy, and never could my heart recognize the great wisdom of Solomon.

After the garments mentioned above had lain for five years in my sleeping chamber, and I did not know what they were suitable for, I finally thought of burning them to clean up the place. And then I spent the whole day going around with such thoughts.

But the next night, there appeared to me in my dream the hundred-year-old woman, and she spoke harshly to me thus: "Thou ungrateful man: for five years I have entrusted to thee my daughter's garments; among them are her most precious jewels, and during all that time thou hast neither cleaned them nor thrown out of them the moths and worms, and now, finally, thou dost want to burn these clothes, and is it not enough that thou art the reason for the death and perishing of my daughter?"

After that, I became hot-headed and answered her: "How shall I understand thee, that thou wouldst make a murderer of me? For five years, my eyes have not beheld thy daughter, and not the least did I hear of her; how then can I be the cause of her death?"

But she would not let me finish and said: "It is all true, but thou hast sinned against God. Therefore, thou could not obtain my daughter, nor the philosophical lixivium I promised thee for washing and cleaning her garments: for in the beginning, when Solomon willingly gave thee my daughter. And when thou didst abhor her garments, that made furious the Planet Saturn, who is her grandfather, and so full of wrath was he that he transformed her again into what she had been before her birth; and since you infuriated Saturn through thine abhorring, thou didst cause her death, putrefaction, and her final destruction, for she is the one of whom Senior saith: Ah, woe! to bring a nude woman unto me, when my first body was not good to look upon, and I had never been mother until I was born again, then I brought forth the power of all roots of herbs, and in mine innermost being I was victorious."

Such heartbreaking words were very strange to me. Still, nevertheless, I withheld my indignation as much as was humanly possible for me, at the same time protesting dignifiedly against her sayings: that I knew nothing at all about her daughter, much less about her death and putrefaction, and although I kept her garments for five years in my sleeping-chamber, I did not know them for my great blindness nor ever discovered their use, and therefore I was innocent before God and all others.

This, my righteous and well-founded excuse, must have pleased the old woman, for she looked at me and said: "I feel and observe from thy righteous mind that thou art innocent, and thine innocence shall be rewarded well and plentifully. Therefore, I will reveal to thee secretly and out of my good heart, namely that my daughter, out of special love and affection towards thee, hath left thee a grey marbled casket as an inheritance amongst her garments, which is covered with a rough, black, dirty case (and meanwhile she gave me a glass filled with lye, and continued speaking), this same little casket thou shalt clean from its stench and dirt which it hath received from the garments. Thou have no need for a key, but it will open itself. Thou wilt find two things therein: a white silver box, filled with magnificent ground-lead and polished diamonds, and another work of art, adorned with costly solar rubies: and this is the treasure and entire legacy of my deceased daughter which she left for thee to inherit before her transformation. Suppose thou wilt only transfer this treasure and purify it most highly and silently and lock it up with great patience in a warm, hidden, steamy, transparent, and moist cellar and protect it from freezing, hail, quick lightning, hot thunder, and other outward destruction till the wheat harvest. In that case, thou wilt first perceive the entire glory of thine inheritance and take part in it."

Meanwhile, I awoke for a second time and called upon God, full of fear, praying that He would open mine, understanding that I might seek the casket that was promised me in my dream. After my prayer had ended, I pursued with the greatest diligence in the garments and found the casket. Still, the casing was tight around it and seemed to have grown onto it by Nature, so I could not take it off. I could not clean it with any lye or split it with iron, steel, or other metal. I left it alone once more and did not know what to do with it, and held it to be witchcraft, thinking of the Prophet's saying: For though thou wash thee with lye, and take thee much soap, yet thine iniquity is marked before me, saith the Lord God.

After a year had passed again and I did not know, after speculating and industriously deliberating, how to remove the casing, I finally went to walk in the garden to rid myself of the melancholy thoughts. After long promenading, I sat down on a flinty stone and fell into a deep sleep. I slept, but my heart was awake: the hundred-year-old stewardess appeared and said: "Hast thou received my daughter's inheritance?"

In a sad voice, I answered, "No, though I found the casket, alone it is still impossible for me to separate the casing, and the lye thou hast given me will not work on it."

After this simple speech, the old woman smiled and said: "Dost thou want to eat shells and shellfish with the shells? Do they not have to be brought forth and prepared by the ancient planet and cook Vulcan? I told thee to thoroughly clean the grey casket with the lye given thee, which proceeded wholly from it and was not refined from the outer rough casing. This thou hast to burn in the fire of the philosophers, then everything will turn out for the best."

And thereupon, she gave me several glowing coals wrapped up in light white taffeta, instructed me further, and pointed out that I should make a philosophical and artful fire and burn the casing. I would soon find the grey casket. And presently, north and south winds rose every hour, sweeping simultaneously through the garden. After that, I awoke, rubbed the sleep out of my eyes, and noticed the glowing coals wrapped in white taffeta lay at my feet. With haste and joy, I grasped them, prayed diligently, called upon God, studied, and labored day and night, and thought meanwhile of the great and excellent sayings of the Philosophers, who say: 'Ignis et azoth tibi sufficient.'

About this, Esdras saith in his fourth book: 'And he gave unto me a full cup which was full of fire, and his form was as of fire. And when I had drunk of it, my heart uttered understanding, and wisdom grew in my breast, for my spirit retained its memory: and my mouth was opened and shut no more. The Most High gave understanding unto the five men, and they wrote, by course, the things that were told them in characters they did not know. So, in forty days were written 204 books, 70 for the wisest alone, who were truly worthy of it, and all were written on boxwood.'

And then I proceeded in silence, as the old woman had revealed to me in my dream until, according to Solomon's prediction, my knowledge became silver, and my memory became golden after a long time. But according to the instructions and teaching of the old stewardess, I enclosed and locked up in a proper and quite artistic manner the treasure of her daughter, namely the splendid and brilliant lunar diamonds and the solar rubies, both of which came forth and were found from the casket and the landscape.

I heard Solomon's voice: "My beloved is white and ruddy, the chiefest among ten thousand. His head is as the finest gold, his locks are bushy, and black as a raven. His eyes are like the eyes of doves by the rivers of waters, washed with milk and fitly set. His cheeks are like a bed of spices, sweet flowers; his lips are like roses, dropping sweet-smelling myrrh. His hands are like gold rings set with the beryl; his belly is as bright ivory overlaid with sapphires. His legs are as pillars of marble, set upon sockets of fine gold; his countenance is as Lebanon, excellent as the cedars. His mouth is most sweet: yea, he is altogether lovely. This is my beloved, and this is my friend, O daughters of Jerusalem. Therefore, shalt thou hold him and not let him go until thou bring him into his mother's house and into his mother's chamber."

And when Solomon had spoken these words, I knew not how to answer him, and I became silent. Still, I wanted to open the locked-up treasure again, with which I might remain unharmed. Then I heard another voice: "I charge you, O ye daughters of Jerusalem, by the roes, and by the hinds of the field, that ye stir not up, nor awake my love, till she please, for she is a garden enclosed, a spring shut up, a fountain sealed, the vineyard at Baal-Hamon, the vineyard at Engeddi, the garden of fruits and spices, the mountain of myrrh, the hill of frankincense, the bed, the litter, the crown, the palm-tree and apple-tree, the flower of Sharon, the sapphire, the turquoise, the wall, tower, and rampart, the garden of joy, the well in the garden, the spring of living water, the king's daughter, and the love of Solomon in his concupiscence: she is the dearest to her mother, and the chosen of her mother, but her head is filled with dew, and her locks with the drops of the night."

Through this discourse and revelation, I was so informed that I knew the purpose of the Wise and did not touch the locked treasure until the work of my own hands, the work was happily completed through God's mercy, the work of noble Nature, and the work of my own hands.

Shortly after this time, just on the day of the month when the moon was new, there occurred an eclipse of the sun, showing itself in all its terrifying power, in the beginning, dark green and some mixed colors, until it finally became coal-black, darkened heaven and earth. Many people were afraid, but I rejoiced, thinking of God's great mercy and the new birth, as Christ Himself pointed out, that a grain of wheat must be cast into the ground, that it may not rot therein, or else it brings forth no fruit.

And then it happened that the darkness was covered with clouds. The sun began to shine through, yet at the same time, three parts of it were still heavily darkened. Lo, an arm broke through the clouds, and my body trembled because of it. It held in its hand a letter with four seals hanging down from it, on which stood written: 'I am black but comely, O ye daughters of Jerusalem, as the tents of Kedar, as the curtains of Solomon: Look not upon me, because I am black because the sun hath looked upon me, etc. But a rainbow spanned itself as soon as the fixed acted in the humid.

I thought of the covenant of the Highest. Of the fidelity of my Doctors and of what I had learned, the sun overcame the darkness with the help of the planet and the fixed stars. Over every mountain and valley, there came a lovely and bright day. All fear and terror had an end, and everything beheld this day and rejoiced, praised the Lord, and said: The winter is past, the rain is over and gone; the flowers appear on the earth; the time of the singing of birds has come, and the voice of the turtle is heard in our land; the fig tree puts forth her green figs and the vines with the tender grape give a good smell. Therefore, let us make haste to take the little foxes that spoil the vines so that we may gather the grapes in time and with them make and drink wine, and be fed at the right time with milk and honeycomb, that we may eat and be filled. And heaven grew pale after the day was done and the evening fell. The seven stars rose with yellow rays and pursued their natural courses through the night until, in the morning, they were overshadowed by the breaking of the sun's red dawn.

And behold, the Wise who dwelt in the land arose from their slumber, looked heavenward, and said: Who is she that looks forth as the morning, fair as the moon, clear as the sun, and there is no spot in her, for her ardor is fiery and not unlike a flame of the Lord: so that no water may extinguish the love, nor any river drowns it; therefore we will not leave her, for she is our sister, and though she is yet little, and hath no breasts, we will bring her again into her mother's house, into a shining hall, where she hath been before, to suck her mother's breasts. Then she will come forth like a tower of David, built with ramparts whereon hang a thousand shields, and many arms of the mighty men; and as she went on the daughter praised her openly, and the queens and the concubines spoke well of her: but I fell upon my face, thanked God, and praised His Holy Name.'

Epilogue

And thus, is brought to a close, ye beloved and faithful Sapientiae et doctrinae filii, in all its power and its glory, the great secret of the Wise, and the revelation of the Spirit, about which the Prince and Monarch Theoph. in the Apocalypse of Hermes says: 'It is a single Numen, a divine, wondrous, and holy office, while it encloses the whole world within it, and will become true with all else, and truly overcomes the elements and the five substances. Eye hath not seen, nor ear heard, neither have entered the heart of any man, how the heaven hath naturally embodied to the truth of this Spirit, in it the truth doth stand alone, therefore it is called: the voice of truth. To this power, Adam and the other patriarchs, Abraham, Isaac, and Jacob, owed their bodily health and long life and finally prospered in great wealth.

With the aid of this Spirit, the Philosophers founded the seven free arts and acquired their wealth in addition to that. With it, Noah built the Ark, Moses the Tabernacle, and Solomon the Temple. He provided the golden vessels made from pure gold in the Temple. For the glory of God, Solomon also wrought with it many fine works and did other great deeds.

With it, Esdras again established the Commandment; with it, Miriam, the sister of Moses, was hospitable. And this Spirit was much used and very common amongst the prophets of the Old Testament. Likewise, it is a medicine, a cure for all things, and the final revelation, the final and highest secret of Nature.

The Spirit of the Lord hath filled the sphere of the earthly kingdom and moved upon the face of the waters in the beginning. The world could neither understand nor grasp it without the Holy Ghost's secret gracious inspiration or teaching. For the whole world longs for it because of its extraordinary powers, which men cannot appreciate enough, and for which the saints have sought from the world's creation and have fervently desired to see.

For this Spirit goes into the seven planets, raises the clouds, and dispels the mists, gives light to all things, transforms everything into gold and silver, giveth health and abundance, treasures, cleans leprosy, cures dropsy and gout, clears the face, prolongs life, strengthens the sorrowful, heals the sick and all the afflicted, yea, it is a secret of all secrets, one secret thing of all secret things, and healing and medicine for all things.

Likewise, it is and remains unfathomable in Nature. Endless power and an invincible might and glory that is a passionate craving for knowledge, and a lovely thing of all things which are beneath the circle of the moon, with which Nature is made strong, and the heart with all members is renewed, and kept in blossoming youth, age is driven away, weakness destroyed, and the entire world refreshed.

Likewise, this Spirit is a spirit chosen above all other heavenly things or spirits, which giveth health, luck, joy, peace, love, expelling altogether all evil, destroying poverty and misery, and also causing that one can neither talk nor think evil; it giveth to men what they desire from the depths of their hearts, worldly honor, and long life to the godly, but eternal punishment to the evil-doers, who put it to improper use.

To the Highest, Almighty God who hath created this art and who hath also been pleased to reveal this knowledge unto me, a miserable, sinful man, through a promise and faithful vow, to Him be given praise, honor, glory, and thanks, with an entirely humble and fervent prayer that He will direct my heart, mind, and senses through His Holy Ghost, so governing that I talk to no one about this secret, much less communicate it to someone who doth not fear God, nor reveal it to any other creature, lest I break my vow and oath, and break the heavenly seals, and thus become a perjured Brother Aurae Crucis, and utterly offend the Divine Majesty, and thereby commit and perpetrate knowingly an unpardonable mighty sin against the Holy Ghost. Wherefore may God the Father, Son, and Holy Ghost, the Most Blessed Trinity, constantly preserve and protect me. Amen. Amen. Amen."

"The 'union of irreconcilables:' marriage of water and fire. The two figures each have four hands to symbolize their many different capabilities." Carl Gustav Jung

Parabola, by Henricus Madathanus, ca 1630

The famous psychiatrist C. G. Jung believed that mental and vital energy is created through the conflict of opposites. According to Jung, the alchemical attempt to transmute base metals into gold and silver (with the help of the philosopher's stone) was essentially a psychological process. He argued that the symbols used by alchemists represented what he termed the process of individuation: personal growth and full integration and mastery of conflicting functions within our conscious, subconscious, and unconscious mind. One must bring the opposites into balance and complete union to gain emotional and physical health and to succeed in the integration of the conscious, subconscious, and unconscious mind, after which one's true Self emerges.

What Jung sees as merely psychological archetypes and symbolic representations of psychological dynamics, modern alchemists consider as the interaction between the spirit of nature and the human spirit-psycho-physical constitution.

In alchemy, the 'uniting of the opposites' is known as the 'coniunctio,' or the Royal Wedding. This represents the union of opposites, specifically the union of Queen and King, anima and animus, our inner male and female aspects, and the wedding between our soul and the spirit of nature. As a result, one's inner and outer life becomes integrated and balanced, and one enters into a state of great peace, tranquility, wisdom, love, empowerment, youthfulness, and health. Jung claims that this is the pure gold (King) and silver (Queen) that the alchemists sought to create with the help of the Philosopher's Stone (black water).

To succeed in this process, the inner animal nature, represented by the lion, has to be first acknowledged and then tamed (brought under the control of the human spirit), and body and mind have to go through destruction (illness, crisis) and metaphysical death and resurrection (developing new faculties, the birth of the higher Self, renewed vitality, and resilience), a process of purification and empowerment.

The bridegroom represents everything connected with red blood and the 'Tree of Knowledge.' The bride signifies all the processes related to blue blood and the transformation of the 'Tree of Death' into the 'Tree of Life.' The newborn royal couple symbolizes the intertwining of the 'Tree of Knowledge' with the 'Tree of Life,' a reflection of our higher developed humanity.

"The Parabola," a Rosicrucian writing by Madathanus, provides a miniature image of the initiation path of Christian Rosenkreuz, as outlined in allegorical images in the "Chymical Wedding of Christian Rosenkreuz" by Johannes Valentino Andreae, first published in 1616, but likely enacted 150 years earlier. The events of this story span seven days and are divided into seven chapters, each relating to a different day. The story begins on an evening near Easter. In the final chapter—the seventh day—Rosenkreuz was knighted in 1459.

"Once upon a time, I was walking in a beautiful, green, and young wood, and there I began to think deeply about the hardships of this life and how much suffering there is in the world, and I felt such deep sorrow. I left the common path, and I came, I know not how, upon a narrow footpath, very rough, untrodden, and hard to walk upon. Which was overgrown with many bushes and shrubs, and it was easy for me to see that this trail had been little used. I became frightened, and I wanted to turn around and go back. Still, it was not within my power, especially since a strong wind blew mightily behind me. Hence, I had to take 10 steps ahead for everyone that I could take backward. So, I had to continue on this trail despite its roughness.

Now, after I had walked for some length of time, I came to a lovely meadow surrounded by a beautiful circle of fruit trees. In this meadow, I met with a group of old men, all of whom had snow-white beards except for one young man with a pointed black beard and another even younger man whom I recognized even though I could not see his face. They were having a huge debate about all kinds of things, especially an essential secret they said the great Creator had hidden deeply within the heart of nature and could only be revealed to those with deeply loving hearts searching for the truth. I listened to them for a long time. I enjoyed hearing their conversations and debates about various subjects, from the arts to the sciences and mathematics. However, I must admit I found some more interesting than others. Then, I realized that they were inspired by the great Greek and Roman philosophers. I could no longer contain myself and express my thoughts about these subjects and what I had learned through my life experiences. Many listened to me and questioned me intensely. They seemed amazed at how good my foundation in philosophy was and at the breadth of my life's experience. They all agreed to take me into their school, and I felt delighted. They said I could not become their real colleague until I first became acquainted with their Lion and understood what he could do to me internally and externally. They told me to do my best to try taming him, and as I longed to be part of their company, I promised, with confidence, to do so. They led me to the Lion and described him to me very carefully.

But nobody could tell me what I had to do with this wild beast. Some tried to help me, but I felt so confused by their suggestions. I could not understand what they were saying, so I finally decided to tie up the Lion and ensure that his sharp claws and pointed teeth could not harm me. after doing so, I finally understood what they were saying when they spoke to me again. The Lion was ancient, ferocious, and big, and his yellow mane hung over his neck. He seemed unconquerable, and I felt so terrified that I would gladly have turned back but for the fact that I had agreed to do this. The old men were standing around me, watching my every move. I confidently approached the Lion in his den and began to humor him. Still, he glared at me so intensely and unceasingly that I soon felt frightened. At the same time, I remembered having heard from an old man on our way to the Lion's den that although very many people had undertaken to conquer the Lion, very few had really done so.

I did not want to fail, and I remembered many grips I had learned through great diligence in my athletics training; I was also so well acquainted with the art of sorcery that I began to feel more confident, and I stopped trying to humor him. And so, I decided to attack the Lion so skillfully and with such great cunning that I could squeeze the blood from his body and even out of his heart before he realized it. And I noticed that his blood was beautifully red and that it was full of bile. Looking further into his anatomy, I found many things I wondered about, especially his bones, which were as white as snow. I noticed that there were a lot more bones than blood. When my dear old men, standing around the den and watching me, became aware of what I had done, they began arguing intensely.

At first, I could not hear exactly what they were saying, as I was so deeply inside the Lion's den. Still, eventually, when they began to shout at one another, I heard one say: He must bring the Lion back to life, or he cannot be part of our school. I did not want to cause more trouble, so I left them and went across a great square and came to a huge wall over four feet high yet only six inches wide. From where I stood beside the wall until the end of it, an iron rail well secured with many supports ran. So, I began walking to the top of the wall and thought I noticed someone else walking ahead of me on the right side of the rail. After following this person for some time, I noticed someone following me on the other side of the rail. I was not sure whether it was a man or a woman who called me and said it would be better for me to walk on their side than where I was going. I agreed to do so straight away, for the handrail that stood in the middle made the path on my side very narrow, and it was hard to walk at such a height. And then I saw some people behind me who wanted to go the same way. So, I swung myself under the rail, grasping it tightly with both hands and continued on the other side until I finally came to a place on the wall where it was dangerous to descend. Then I wished I had stayed on the other side, for I could not pass under the rail again, and it was also impossible for me to turn back and retake the other way. Therefore, I took a chance, trusted my good feet, held on tightly, and came down without harm.

When I had walked on for some time, I soon forgot about the danger, and I also did not know what became of the wall or the handrail. And when I did come down, there stood in front of me a beautiful rose bush, which grew the most exquisite white and red roses. I noticed more red than white ones, broke some of them off, and put them on my hat. Then, I became aware of a wall enclosing a great garden. And in the garden, there were many young men, and I knew there must also be many young women who would like to join them there but who would not have been able to walk around the wall and find the door. I felt sorry for them, so I returned the way I had come to look for them, and I walked on so quickly that I soon reached several houses, one of which I hoped would belong to the gardener. I met many people there; each one had a special place where they worked, and I noticed two of them in particular working very carefully and slowly together. Although each person had his own field of work, I felt I had done all these things before and knew more than all. I felt a kind of freedom deep inside. And so, I did not want to remain there any longer because I found their work so meaningless, and I was determined to go further.

As I approached the garden door, some people looked at me with such bitterness that I feared they would prevent me from going further. But others said, "See how he wants to go into the garden, and yet we who have worked here for so long dare not enter it. Let us only mock him if he fails." But I ignored them because I knew more about the garden than they did. Although I had never been into it, I went right up to a door that was locked tightly and did not appear to have a keyhole on the outside of it. I noticed a small round hole in the door, hidden from the naked eye, and I knew this was the way to get inside, so I took out my master key, prepared myself, unlocked the door, and entered.

Once inside, I found more locked doors and opened them all without trouble. I found myself in a passageway covered by a ceiling, and it seemed that I was inside a well-constructed house, about six feet wide and twenty feet long. Although all the other doors were still locked, I could see clearly into the garden when I opened the first door. With courage, I walked further on and into the garden. In the middle of it, I soon discovered a much smaller square garden, which was square in shape (and only measured 180 square yards on each side). It was covered with wild rose bushes, which were blossoming beautifully. And as it had rained a little and the sun shone, there was a beautiful rainbow. When I left the little garden, I arrived at the place where I knew I could help the young women. I noticed that a low fence made of wooden twigs stood instead of the walls. There, I saw a most beautiful young woman dressed in white satin and accompanied by an equally handsome young man leading her by the arm and walking past the rose garden, carrying many fragrant roses in their hands. I spoke to them, and I asked them: how did you get over the fence? And she said: my dearest bridegroom helped me over it, and we are now going out of this lovely garden and into our bedroom to consummate our marriage. I told them I was pleased that they could be happy together without my helping them any longer. But I also needed them to know that I had come a long way and I had worked very hard indeed to be of service to them.

After this meeting, I came to a great mill built of stones. I could not see any flour bins or other milling materials. And I observed that not one of the water wheels was turning. I asked the old miller why, and he told me all the milling machinery was locked up on the other side of the building. As I saw the miller's servant going in that direction, I followed him. And I found myself in a passageway with the water wheels above my head. The water appeared to be as back as coal, and the drops of water moving around the wheels were as white as snow. The passageway where I stood was no wider than three of my fingers put together. Nevertheless, I took a risk, held onto the wheel above my head, and crossed the water without getting wet. Then I asked the miller how many water wheels he had. Then, he answered. I knew I would never forget this adventure and longed to discover what it all meant.

I left when I realized the miller did not want to speak to me anymore. I found myself in front of the mill, where there was a high hill covered with paving stones, and on top of the hill, I recognized some old men with white beards walking in the warm sunshine. They held a letter in their hands, which was written by the whole school, and the contents they were discussing. I knew that this letter was probably about me, so I went up to them and asked them directly: Sirs, is this letter about me? Yes, they said, and they told me that I had to keep faithful to my wife and to my marriage, which had just taken place, or they would report it to the authorities. And I answered: that would be very easy for me to do as it was almost as if we were twin souls born at the same moment, and as if we had shared the same childhood and because we had shared so much intimacy, I would always feel bound to my wife until the day I died for I loved her with all my heart. They replied, we have nothing to worry about as the bride feels the same as you, so you will always be joined together. And I told them how happy I felt about these things.

Then, one of them said that if this happened, the Lion would return to life and be more mighty and powerful. And when I thought about how hard I had worked already, for some strange reason, I felt that this task I was being asked to undertake did not belong to me. And so, as I watched the bridegroom and his bride, dressed so beautifully, walking away from me, all ready and prepared to be married, I felt relieved. And at the moment when the bridegroom dressed in his bright scarlet red clothes walked towards the old man with his beloved bride, whose white satin dress shone in the sunlight, They were joined together, it was as if the bride seemed completely ageless and as if she carried the secret of eternal youth.

But it seemed that this man and this woman had done something terribly wrong. It was as though they had become so close that they were now locked in a relationship that was harming both of them. So, instead of sharing a bridal bed and a true marriage, they were now condemned for the rest of their lives to endure a painful existence in which they would have to face themselves. But because they had such noble hearts and to stop them from hiding anything anymore, they were placed in an almost transparent prison made of crystal and shaped like a great dome that seemed to be open to the skies. Before entering this room, they removed all their clothes and jewelry. So, they lived there naked, alone, and utterly vulnerable without any possessions. All the food and drink they needed came from the water mill and were made available. The door of this chamber was well locked, and it had the seal of our school placed upon it, and no one was allowed to enter.

I was told to guard the door, and as winter was approaching, I must heat their room so they should neither freeze nor burn, and I must never allow them to escape. I was given my orders, and if anything went wrong, I was told I would be severely punished. I felt very uneasy, so worried and frightened that I lost my courage. But I knew that there was nothing I could do. I was being tested, and I was determined not to fail. The room in which they were locked was located in the middle of a strong tower surrounded by high walls and fortifications, which one could heat with a moderate but constant fire.

And so began my work to protect the imprisoned married couple from the cold.

But what happened was that as soon as they felt the slightest warmth, they embraced each other in the most loving way possible. And they clung to each other with such ardent passion that the bridegroom's entire body melted and seemed to fall apart in the arms of his beloved wife. And when the bride who loved him as deeply as he loved her saw what had happened, she wept so deeply that her tears covered his whole body and completely buried him. She only cried for a short time, and then her heart broke in two, and she died of sorrow.

Poor me, I found myself in a state of fear, pain, and extreme misery because the two whom I was supposed to be guarding seemed to have dissolved entirely into the water and lay before me as if they were dead. I was confronted with my failure, and what seemed worst of all was that I would not only be ridiculed, but my life would almost certainly be in danger. I spent many days thinking carefully about what I could do. I remembered the story of the Greek princess Medea, who brought the hero Jason back to life again. And I thought to myself: if Medea could do this, why should I not be able to do this also?

I began to think about how I could begin. I thought that the first step would be to maintain the steady warmth in the room so that the water could dissolve, and then I would be able to see the dead bodies of the lovers again. I hoped I could escape from danger and even win praise for my work, so I continued to warm the room with constant heat for forty days. I noticed that, gradually, the water began to disappear. Finally, I could see the dead bodies, which had become as black as coal. Had the room not been so securely sealed and I had been able to go inside, this could have happened sooner.

Then, I noticed that as the water evaporated, it slowly rose to the room's ceiling. When it eventually reached the top, it fell down on the couple again like rain. As no water could actually escape, in front of my very eyes, the bodies of the dead bride and bridegroom began to decay and stink beyond measure. At the same time, I noticed a rainbow appearing in the most beautiful colors caused by the sunshine in this moist environment, which lifted my spirits a little. I still felt happy to see the two lovers again. Joy is always accompanied by pain, and I also felt sorrowful when I saw the ones I was supposed to be looking after lying dead before me. As they lay in a strongly fortified place, I had confidence that their souls and spirits could not escape. So, I continued to work faithfully, creating a constant warmth for them day and night, and imagining that their souls and spirits would eventually return to their bodies once the dampness had passed. I discovered that this was indeed true. And I observed that in the evenings, after some time, it was as if the sun drew up all the vapors from this room and that during the night, they changed into a lovely and fertile dew which came down again in the morning moistening and washing their dead bodies and making them even more white and beautiful again. And the whiter and more beautiful the bride and bridegroom became, the more their bodies dried out and when all the dampness in the room had disappeared.

Finally, the air was light and clear; firstly, the spirit and soul of the bride could no longer remain in the air. They returned to her body, and she became utterly transformed and even more beautiful. And instantly, she came to life again. I felt unbelievably happy, especially when she stood up. I noticed she was wearing the most exquisite dress I had ever seen and was adorned with a crown of perfect diamonds. As she rose, she said: 'I have a message to give all human beings. We are in the hands of the Great Creator; one moment, we may be rich, and another, we can become poor, die, and be reborn. I can testify to this. I was great, and I became small, and when I felt most humble, I was raised and made a queen of many realms. I died, and now I am reborn. And I have gained great wisdom through these experiences. And I have been given the power to make the poor rich, offer mercy to the humble, and bring health to the sick. But I am not the same as my beloved brother, the great and mighty King, who will soon return to life. He will be the living proof of everything I am saying to you when reborn.'

And as she spoke, the sun shone brightly, and the days became warmer, and soon it was the hottest time of the year. So, we prepared for the wedding of our new queen and made the most exquisite dresses for her of black velvet, ash-colored damask, grey silk, silver-colored taffeta, and snow-white satin. The silver was stunning, embroidered with priceless pearls, and covered with the most perfect glittering diamonds. And with the same amount of care, we prepared garments for the young King. Some were pink with threads of pure gold woven through them, and there was one red velvet cloak lavishly adorned with rubies and garnets. But the tailors who made these garments were invisible as no one else had entered the chamber besides the bride and bridegroom. I was amazed to see these garments appearing as if out of nowhere. What was most astonishing was that the others disappeared before my eyes as soon as one coat or dress was ready. I did not know whether they had vanished or whether someone had locked them away.

When the most splendid coats were ready, the bridegroom, who had become a great and mighty King, appeared in all his magnificence, and there was no one in the world as handsome as he was. When he realized he was locked in, he asked me in a friendly and courteous way to open the door so he could go out. And he said he would reward me if I did so. Although I had been strictly forbidden to open the chamber, I felt so overwhelmed by his mighty presence that he managed to persuade me, and I opened the door willingly. And he left in such a dignified yet humble manner. He emanated such goodwill that I recognized instantly that he had a truly noble heart. And as he had spent all these hottest days in such great heat, he was very thirsty, weak, and tired and asked me to bring him some of the running water from under the water wheels of the mill.

I did this, and after he had quenched his great thirst, he returned to the room and told me to lock the door securely behind him as he did not want to be disturbed or woken up when he was deeply asleep. He rested there for several days, then asked me to open the door one day. Then I noticed he had become completely revitalized and was even more handsome and self-possessed. At this point, he said his health was due entirely to drinking such marvelous and healthy water. And so, he ordered more and drank even more than before. At the same time, I decided to build the chamber even bigger.

And when the King had finished drinking as much as he wanted, he became the most handsome and noble human being that I have ever seen in my entire life. Then he led me into his kingdom and showed me all the treasures and riches of the world. And I realized he and his queen were prepared to share their wisdom and riches with those ready to receive it. And there was an abundance of gold and precious stones made available for the well-being of all. Good health was restored, and it became possible to cure all diseases. And finally, in this kingdom, the greatest joy was that the human beings who lived there could rest in the knowledge that a great love existed that embraced them all."

Paracelsus

Philippus Aureolus Theophrastus Bombastus von Hohenheim, known as Paracelsus (*probably late 1493 in Einsiedeln, Switzerland; †September 24, 1541, in Salzburg), was a multifaceted figure: a physician, alchemist, astrologer, mystic, lay theologian, and philosopher.

Today, Paracelsus is recognized as a physician and chemist who introduced groundbreaking ideas and opposed the widely accepted humoral theory based on Galen's teachings. His medical system incorporated elements of alchemy, astrology, mysticism, and hands-on experience. He confidently and independently advocated for his views against the medical establishment of his time, famously declaring, "Let no man belong to another who can belong to himself." His criticism of academic physicians, whom he viewed as inexperienced and disconnected from reality, was often sharp. He recognized that many diseases stem from external influences and can be countered with chemical substances, thus amassing significant pharmaceutical knowledge during his era. Much of his work was only printed posthumously, and he remained largely unknown during his lifetime. He published his knowledge in over 500 writings.

Paracelsus frequently had to defend himself in court due to his controversial views and methods. He was occasionally accused of administering poison to his patients. In his defense, he made the renowned statement: "All things are poison, and nothing is without poison; only the dose permits something not to be poisonous," often paraphrased as "The dose makes the poison."

The doctrine of signatures is also attributed to Paracelsus. He invented the opium tincture known as Laudanum, which was long considered a universal remedy. Additionally, he created Opodeldoc.

Paracelsus was the son of Wilhelm, an illegitimate descendant of the Swabian minor nobility family of the Bombaste von Hohenheim. His father, a physician and chemist, was his first teacher. Paracelsus later studied chemistry and alchemy under the guidance of Abbot Johannes Trithemius at the Sponheim monastery and the wound healer Fugger.

After expanding his knowledge through extensive travels, Paracelsus became renowned in Germany for his treatments. In 1526, he was appointed the city physician in Basel and lectured at the local university. Demonstrating his leadership in medicine, he publicly burned the works of the Greek physician Galen and the Oriental physician Avicenna.

Following a dispute with the Basel city council in 1528, Paracelsus led a nomadic life through Alsace, Switzerland, and southern Germany, until his death in 1541 in Salzburg. His tomb remains in St. Sebastian's Church there.

According to Paracelsus, medicine is fundamentally about understanding nature and God. He believed that true comprehension of diseases and their treatment comes not only from empirical findings but also from contemplating the whole: "For man can only be universally grasped from the Macrocosm, not from within himself. Only knowledge of this correspondence completes the physician" (Opus Paramirum).

For Paracelsus, the material body was just a part of the complete body, mostly invisible to the ordinary observer. He posited that those who engaged in constant self-work (inner transformation) and attained divine enlightenment could perceive the world "in the light of nature" (Opus Paramirum). Such individuals, he argued, were the only ones fit to be physicians because "It is wrong to draw one's knowledge in medicine from hearsay and reading... The natural force in fire should also be our teacher" and "But fire makes visible what is otherwise in the dark. Science should be presented according to this method" (Opus Paramirum). According to Paracelsus, the successful practice of medical art required not only knowledge and mastery of four sub-disciplines but also God's grace.

These sub-disciplines include:

1. Philosophy (love of wisdom; not to be confused with modern philosophy): Paracelsus believed that a true philosopher should

"combine Heaven and Earth in a Microcosm" to guard against falsehood and ground their understanding in a holistic view of the universe.

2. Astronomy (the science of the inner planets and stars; not to be confused with modern astronomical science): According to Paracelsus, "Astronomy is the second foundation and represents the upper sphere of philosophy," essential for comprehending a person in their entire composition.

3. Alchemy: He described alchemy as the art required to complete nature's unfinished processes: "For nature is so subtle and sharp that it cannot be applied without great art. It does not bring forth anything that would be complete, but man must complete it. This completion is called Alchemy." He also emphasized the importance of learning Spagyria, which teaches the separation of the false from the righteous.

4. Proprietas (honesty): Paracelsus stressed the virtue of honesty for physicians, linking it to faith: "Therefore, the physician of the people should possess faith, so he has it also with God."

Paracelsus also identified five main types of disease influences, referred to as Entia, which include:

- Ens Astrorum or Ens Astrale: Influences of the planets and stars.
- Ens Veneni: Poisons absorbed by the body.
- Ens Naturale: Predetermined factors, such as one's constitution.
- Ens Spirituale: Influences of spirits.
- Ens Dei: Direct influences of God.

These elements form the foundation of Paracelsus's medical philosophy, emphasizing a comprehensive understanding of both the material and spiritual aspects of health.

According to Paracelsus, every disease can be traced back to one or more of five primary causes, which he called Entia. For instance, the effects of a poison (Ens Veneni) can be exacerbated by a weak constitution (Ens Naturale). Thus, for an accurate diagnosis, a physician must consider the totality of these influences.

Paracelsus identified three fundamental substances—'Sulphur,' 'Mercury,' and 'Salt'—as essential components of the body. He believed that disease results from imbalances among these substances and that healing involves restoring this equilibrium. This could be achieved, for example, by administering remedies that possess the required properties to counteract the imbalances.

In his practice, Paracelsus not only utilized but also refined traditional healing methods. He applied the doctrine of signatures, a belief that the physical forms of objects in the natural world indicate their potential therapeutic uses, to identify medicinal substances. He further employed alchemical techniques to extract their active ingredients. Paracelsus grounded his approach in the fundamental hermetic principle of correspondence, which posits a mutual relationship between humans as the Microcosm and the universe as the Macrocosm.

The interpretation of Paracelsus's teachings continues to be a topic of discussion among proponents of both traditional and alternative medicine, reflecting his enduring influence on health and healing practices.

Paracelsus about Alchemy and the Seven Metals

1. To train the doctor

Nature instructs the physician, who must immerse himself in it to learn, for everything originates from and exists within nature. The distinction between nature and philosophy is that philosophy involves studying the world and the cosmos. A philosopher grows through his connections to both the heavens and the earth. From the earth, we derive minerals, ores, and plants, each with their own powers and qualities that the philosopher must understand. Humans are akin to these elements, composed of earth, water, minerals, and plant-like qualities within.

From the heavens, we receive air, fire, and stellar influences. Astronomers, who study the stars' properties, find parallels in humans, who possess their own celestial and chaotic natures. As the spheres are divided in the cosmos, so they are mirrored in humans, where external knowledge enhances internal wisdom. Physicians must comprehend both the celestial and terrestrial realms—their substances, nature, and essence—to effectively initiate treatment. This insight stems from nature's illumination, the source of profound wisdom. A physician draws his knowledge from Nature, his origin, discovering the essence of all bodily organs and their conditions.

Philosophers should anchor their philosophy in this microcosmic summary of heaven and earth, reflecting these in humanity, just as physicians see the macrocosm reflected in individuals.

Our teachings commence with the understanding that humans contain a cosmic counterpart within—a dynamic system of celestial bodies undergoing changes. These cosmic observations should inform and clarify our understanding of the human body. Recognizing these cosmic patterns externally aids physicians in applying these insights internally. The body's influences mirror celestial dynamics, equipping physicians with their greatest skills. By mastering the external macrocosm, the physician gains insights into health and disease, which guide his medical practice.

Indeed, the arts of working with metals and other natural resources derive from celestial bodies yet remain partially undiscovered. Divine design dictates that natural insights are celestial, encouraging humans to learn from them.

A true philosopher understands the origins and properties of metals, plants, and celestial bodies, recognizing their unified essence, despite diverse appearances and names.

Nature itself is imperfect; it is human endeavor to perfect it through the art of alchemy. If one comprehensively understands philosophy, astronomy, diseases, remedies, and their formulations, then mastering the artful preparation of these elements is crucial. It's not merely about physical mixing but activating and applying the inherent powers.

Nature teaches us through its own processes, like transforming grain into seeds or grapes into wine. These transformations are guided by celestial forces, which should also align with medical practices.

Disease, health, and healing are influenced by celestial bodies. Thus, medicine must be prepared in alignment with these cosmic forces, using simple, holistic methods to tap into and harness their power.

Materials must undergo transformation through fire to benefit humanity. In this process, physicians should focus on extracting and refining the active essences, avoiding crude materials to prevent interference with the healing essences.

Therefore, it is crucial to understand that true medicinal power lies in the essences, which are formless, clear, and influenced by celestial dynamics, like chaos moved by the stars.

2. The relationship between planet, metal, and man

Metals deeply resonate with the human body, reflecting a profound connection between the larger universe (macrocosm) and individual beings (microcosm), symbolizing their unified nature.

A fundamental principle of action, often represented as a 'star,' governs everything: in humans, it influences the mind and spirit; in animals, it impacts their senses; and in elements and celestial bodies, it guides their behavior and trajectories. This principle requires a specific arrangement of forces to mediate its impact on different substances and entities. For example, the influence attributed to Mars necessitates a corresponding 'Mars star' or similar agent.

In every entity, there is a structure (anatomy), functionality (essence), and material (matter). Consider the celestial correspondences:

- Seven planets associated with fire,
- Seven metals linked to water,
- Seven herbs connected to earth,
- Seven elements related to air,
- Seven vital organs in living beings.

The celestial force governing a planet bestows unique abilities, a principle that also applies to other domains such as water, air, fire, and living beings.

The universe consists of both tangible elements like planets or metals and intangible aspects like the celestial body (Ens astrale), similar to the human soul, which remains hidden.

1. The celestial body divides into two aspects:
2. The terrestrial star (Ens vitale, or spirit of life) promotes growth from the earth and physical forms.

The celestial star (Ens astrale) influences the mind, governing senses and rationality.

Humans reflect this dual nature, possessing both a visible, physical body made up of elements and organs (like the liver, heart, spleen, and brain) and an invisible, spiritual 'astral body' or soul, from which consciousness and reason emerge.

The seven planets significantly influence their corresponding metals, each embodying specific properties and energies:

- The Sun influences gold,
- Jupiter impacts tin,
- Mercury corresponds with mercury (the element),
- Mars is linked to iron,
- Venus is associated with copper,
- Saturn influences lead,
- The Moon affects silver.

The spiritual essence within metals, similar to the guiding principle in celestial bodies, endows metals with unique properties. Ancient philosophers used the same symbols for the seven metals and the seven planets, highlighting the interconnection between celestial and terrestrial realms.

However, it's essential to recognize that while stars are often described as possessing properties, it is the spirit within them—the Ens astrale—that holds these qualities. This celestial influence over our bodies dictates how each organ receives vitality through its corresponding planetary influence, which directs its function.

For example, the heart, akin to the Sun, distributes its spirit throughout the body, dedicated exclusively to bodily functions without affecting other organs.

- The circulation paths of these spirits are critical:
- The spirit from the brain travels only to the heart and back.
- The liver's spirit circulates within the blood.
- The spleen's spirit lies adjacent to the intestines.
- The kidneys' spirit flows through the urinary system.
- The lungs function within the chest and throat.
- The bile moves through the stomach and intestines.

If these paths are disrupted—such as the spleen's path intruding into that of the bile—illness results. The direction and function of each organ are not dictated by the body itself but by its corresponding celestial influence.

Thus, the efficacy of medicines depends on their alignment with celestial guidance. Without this celestial direction, medicines might remain inactive, merely passing through the digestive system without effecting any healing.

Principle	Planet	Metal	Organ
Saturn	Saturn	Lead	Spleen
Jupiter	Jupiter	Tin	Liver
Martian	Mars	Iron	Bile
Solar	Sun	Gold	Heart
Venus	Venus	Copper	Kidneys
Mercury	Mercury	Mercury	Lung
Moon	Moon	Silver	Genitals, brain

The heavens share a deep connection with humanity, mirroring our primal traits. Just as the stars represent reason, wisdom, cunning, and warfare, so too do humans embody these qualities, deriving them from the celestial realm.

The celestial body acts as humanity's progenitor, from which we originate. These are the Corpora Astralia of the Microcosm, inheriting characteristics from their celestial forebears. For instance, Mars has its counterpart in human nature, as do the other planets.

Stars are of two distinct natures: one earthly and one heavenly, one representing instinct and the other wisdom. The earthly aspects relate to our physical forms and functions, such as the liver, heart, spleen, and brain. The urges to eat and drink arise from these terrestrial elements, which also empower the body to grow and reproduce.

The body processes nutrients from the earth, affected by the unique blend of elements present at conception. In his behaviors and instincts, a person exhibits qualities shared with animals. Depending on his predominant characteristics, a person might demonstrate tendencies similar to those of different animals, such as a cow or a wolf. If a person does not manage his primal instincts, the celestial forces will overpower him, molding his personality to be more driven by desire, sensuality, lust, anger, and similar traits.

3. The cause of the diseases

The heavens are closely linked to humanity, shaping our primal instincts. Just as the stars represent wisdom, cunning, and warfare, we humans exhibit these traits because they originate from celestial forces. In this sense, the celestial realm acts like a progenitor to humanity, passing down the 'Corpora astralia' of the Microcosm— each planet, like Mars, imparts specific influences on the human spirit.

Stars fall into two categories: earthly and heavenly, which correspond to nature (folly) and wisdom, respectively. Earthly elements like the liver, heart, spleen, and brain drive our fundamental needs such as hunger and thirst. In contrast, our higher aspirations are influenced by our soul, which draws nourishment from the celestial realm of its origin. Thus, human perfection is defined by the interplay between our elemental and celestial natures, each with its own tendencies, often to excess.

When the elemental body indulges its basic desires over the guidance of the celestial, it distorts inherent wisdom. This underscores the importance of recognizing who dominates and who is dominated by celestial influences. Indeed, those who fail to manage their inner celestial forces become overwhelmed by these energies, losing control over their actions.

If an individual gives in to their primal mind, opening themselves to lower influences as one might foolishly stare at the sun and become blinded, they fall into vices such as gluttony and lust, losing touch with their humanity. Conversely, the celestial realm, pure and chaste, withdraws from such degradation.

However, when an individual masters their base instincts, they elevate their higher, soulful nature, which then aligns with health-promoting celestial influences from planets like Saturn, Jupiter, and Venus.

Each celestial body affects our physical constitution, potentially cooling or heating our systems, or making them too salty or acidic, mirroring planetary characteristics. These influences can be beneficial or detrimental, highlighting the dual nature of celestial impacts.

The 'rods of heaven'—the stars—can induce diseases based on their interactions with the human body. Therefore, understanding the celestial roots of illnesses is essential, beyond just analyzing symptoms like urine or pulse. Each disease corresponds to a celestial influence that engenders these conditions within us.

Furthermore, mental illnesses such as hysteria, epilepsy, and melancholy stem from various celestial impacts, with each condition traceable to a specific planet that reflects its influence. By understanding this connection, we not only comprehend the nature and origin of diseases but also their potential remedies.

In summary, our behaviors and actions can provoke celestial entities, leading to diseases as forms of retribution. Thus, our well-being is deeply intertwined with the macrocosm, the heavenly domain, influenced by how we conduct our lives in virtue, peace, and love.

4. Healing and the alchemy of the soul

From the celestial realm stem the intangible aspects of sense and reason, along with virtues such as wisdom, power, knowledge, law, arts, and scholarship. The celestial body aims to guide humanity toward profound wisdom and skill, enlightening us through the natural light. This realm encompasses all faculties, arts, and wisdom—it serves as the school from which we learn. For example, the influence of Venus first introduced music, while Mars spurred the development of crafts, illustrating how celestial forces actively nurture various earthly arts.

We derive reason and artistry from the stars, our natural teachers, who instruct us via this natural illumination. Humans have an innate conscience that empowers us to transcend both our celestial and earthly origins, placing our power and judgment in this higher awareness. A wise individual can control the celestial influences, turning them into tools rather than masters, thereby making the heavens serve us.

Even those born under the challenging influence of Saturn can shift their alignment toward the sun, transitioning from illness to health— similar to how the moon's influence can yield to the vitality of the sun. Medicine facilitates this change, symbolizing a move from constraint to liberation, from the sway of a malevolent planet to the guidance of a beneficial one.

God created the planets to assist humanity, not to dominate us, akin to all other natural entities. Metals have a remarkable affinity with the human body, and when properly understood and applied, they support nature. While the seven planets may have adverse effects, the seven metals offer specific remedies for the afflictions associated with these celestial bodies. For example, the Quinta Essentia of gold can counteract solar influences, empowering the heart and offering protection against all celestial forces.

At the heart of medical practice are the Arcana—mystical secrets where wellness is nurtured, and illness defeated. Each metal addresses ailments associated with its celestial counterpart, as Mercury does for mercurial conditions. Just as nature instructs us in order and preparation, we must tailor specific remedies for each ailment.

The laws of the celestial sphere dictate the relationships of all things with humanity. God has endowed the celestial bodies with all natural wisdom and art, charging them with the governance of ephemeral matters. Those who pursue wisdom and art must seek these heavenly sources, for the finest healers are among the planets, safeguarding the art of healing.

The most adept physician understands all diseases and knows the virtues of herbs, metals, and precious stones. Let physicians draw knowledge from these celestial wellsprings, as the ancients once did. We should continuously strive to expand our understanding, explore, and learn beyond traditional boundaries—this pursuit is the essence of true alchemy.

True alchemy is not merely about converting base metals into gold and silver; it aims to enhance and perfect metals. The characteristics of a place can either degrade or enhance a substance; for instance, Jupiter, situated away from Mars and Venus but closer to the Sun and

Moon, shares more properties with gold and silver, enhancing its strength and presence.

Tin, which contains traces of gold and silver, should be sourced from distant locations where these noble metals are spiritually concealed. The alchemist's goal is to elevate the base to the noble, perfecting metals through diverse alchemical processes. This journey from imperfection to perfection represents the true labor of alchemy.

MYSTERIVM MAGNVM
STVDIVM VNIVERSALI

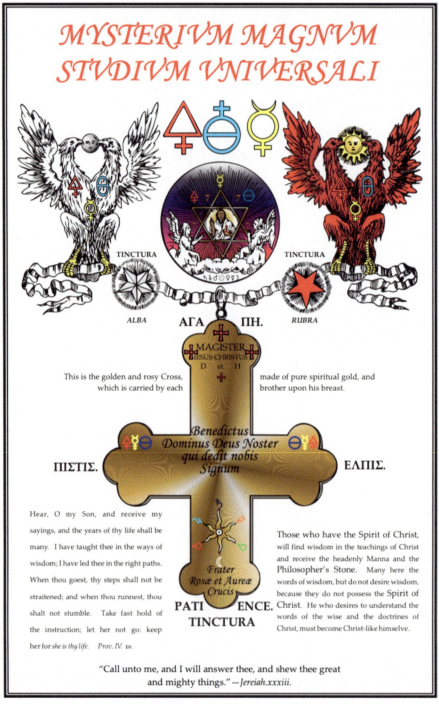

This is the golden and rosy Cross, which is carried by each made of pure spiritual gold, and brother upon his breast.

Hear, O my Son, and receive my sayings, and the years of thy life shall be many. I have taught thee in the ways of wisdom; I have led thee in the right paths. When thou goest, thy steps shall not be straitened; and when thou runnest, thou shalt not stumble. Take fast hold of the instruction; let her not go: keep her for she is thy life. *Prov. IV.* 10.

Those who have the Spirit of Christ, will find wisdom in the teachings of Christ and receive the headenly Manna and the Philosopher's Stone. Many here the words of wisdom, but do not desire wisdom, because they do not possess the Spirit of Christ. He who desires to understand the words of the wise and the doctrines of Christ, must become Christ-like himself.

"Call unto me, and I will answer thee, and shew thee great and mighty things." —*Jereiah.xxxiii.*

From: The Secret Symbols of the Rosicrucians. Altona 1785.

The Seal of Salomon

'Coincidentia oppositorum' is a state or condition in which opposites no longer oppose each other but fall together into harmony, union, or conjunction. A unity of contrarieties overcoming opposition by convergence without destroying or merely blending the constituent element. It sets forth the way God works, the order of things in relation to God and to each other, and how humans may approach and abide in God.

Nicholas of Cusa, 1404 -1464

The Seven Metals and the Philosopher's Stone

Paracelsus argued that a physician should not merely serve nature but transcend it. While a deep understanding of natural processes is essential, a physician must also be an artist, creatively extending what nature begins. Paracelsus envisioned a new era of medicine, suggesting that true remedies arise not from merely extracting substances from nature, but from innovatively crafting products inspired by the spirit of nature. This approach promotes advancing the course of nature rather than adhering to its current state.

In the future, practitioners of spiritual science will embrace a form of chemistry that aligns with the dynamic, evolving aspects of nature, rather than merely mimicking a static version of it. This shift will mark a significant advancement in how we perceive and interact with natural remedies.

Please be aware: The homeopathic remedies described herein are not intended to replace any treatments prescribed by your healthcare professional or therapist. In cases of suspected physical or mental illness, it is essential to consult with a qualified health professional or therapist. If you have any doubts about your health, always seek the advice of your healthcare provider or therapist.

Alloy comp 10 M

Alloy comp is a potentized homeopathic remedy formulated from a blend of six metals: Argentum metallicum (silver), Mercurius vivus (mercury), Cuprum metallicum (copper), Ferrum metallicum (iron), Stannum (tin), and Plumbum metallicum (lead), all prepared in a 10 MK potency. This composition may function as an adaptogen, helping the body adapt to stress and exerting a normalizing effect upon bodily processes. Additionally, it is considered a polycrest, meaning it has a wide range of applications in homeopathic medicine and can address multiple health issues.

Treatment Guidelines for Integrated Physicians

- Alloy comp, a homeopathic metal combination, must be prescribed by a doctor trained in anthroposophic, homeopathic, or naturopathic medicine.
- The selection of this remedy at any given time is based on an understanding of the spiritual nature of the remedies and their documented effects, as researched by Rudolf Steiner, Ita Wegman, Hilma Walter, Ala Selawry, Wilhelm Pelikan, among others in the fields of Anthroposophic and homeopathic medicine. It also considers the individual's spirit-psycho-physical constitution.
- If you are experiencing any physical, emotional, or mental health issues, please consult a health professional or qualified therapist before using this remedy.
- Do not use Alloy comp without the explicit permission and guidance of a health professional or qualified therapist. Should you experience any adverse effects while using this remedy, discontinue use immediately.
- Alloy comp 10M is available by prescription only and can be obtained from Ainsworth Pharmacy in London.

For more in-depth information about the relationship of the metals in Alloy comp to the Philosopher's Stone, please refer to my book: 'Gold and the Philosopher's Stone'.

Ita Wegman's Meditation to Connect with Christian Rosenkreuz

(Passed on by Rudolf Steiner)

I hold the Sun within me
As King, he leads me to the world.
I hold the Moon within me.
She preserves my form.
I hold Mercury within me.
He holds Sun and Moon together.

I hold Venus within me.
Without her love all is naught.
She unites herself with Mars,
Who speaks my being in the Word.

That Jupiter may illumine the whole.
With wisdom light.
And Saturn the mature
May ray within the colours of my being.

That's the Seven of the world.
I am the Seven.
I am the world, of the Earth wide.
I am the Sun.

The Hiram Legend

As paraphrased by Rudolf Steiner in The Temple Legend
and narrated by Patrick Dixon

"Solomon raised his mind, just like a plant raises itself above the Earth to receive the inspirations of the Sun, to receive all the wondrous measurements and proportions of points, lines, planes, and angles, of what would become the great Temple { the Temple his Father had not time to build; he opened his heart until it was ready to make real on Earth, the ideal conceived in the heights so that it might be deeply founded on the Earth. To make the ideal a reality, he would need the help of a Master builder and mason, supremely skilled also in metallurgy, carpentry, and glasswork; an artisan who developed to as perfect as humanly possible, all the crafts and arts that had been handed on from his ancestors, to reach in him the most complete expression. This was Hiram Abif.

"On the other side, King Solomon was seen as one who had ascended the peaks of wisdom, from where he could survey all the wonders of the Word in the World and the Worlds in the Word, a poet, peacemaker, and philosopher King. These two working together were as the uniting of two streams that, in ancient times, had diverged from a single source and, ever since, run parallel to each other, but now could be reconciled in a single project, as two dreams that sought to wake to one reality, the Temple.

"At their first meeting, Solomon spoke, saying. 'Hiram, I know you are the only one capable of realizing, in outer form, the vision I have received.'

"Hiram answered: 'I feel honored and shall aim to prove that your choosing me was a wise choice. I feel my destiny and all I have learned have led to this task; the Temple will be the realization, fulfillment, and triumphant climax of all my hands can shape.'

"So, Hiram, with teams of workers, set about building. While this happened, Solomon continued to be a light of wisdom to his subjects, dispensing wise judgments in all state affairs, his thoughts and words bringing healing and harmony amidst all the problems of his peoples' daily lives. As the Temple neared completion, news of its construction and the great Wisdom of Solomon that had made it possible had spread far and wide beyond his Kingdom. It reached the attention of the Queen of Sheba, the legendary ruler of a country south of Egypt on the Nile.

"So moved was the Queen by tales of Solomon's wisdom and the great Temple that she decided to take the long journey to question him, hear his answers, and look upon the marvel of the Temple. After a long and arduous journey, her great caravan, consisting of many servants, camels, horses, and mules laden with gifts of gems, rare fabrics, embroidered silks, and aromatic spices, arrived in Solomon's Kingdom. Somebody informed him of her coming and prepared a welcoming ceremony and a festivity that spared no expense. Upon first seeing her, he exclaimed: 'Your beauty surpasses all the descriptions I have heard.'

"In the following days, she spent most of her time with Solomon, walking in the palace gardens and listening to his words as he answered her many questions.

"She told him, 'In your words, it is as if I hear super earthly music that lifts my mind into harmonies of boundless wonder.'

"Solomon felt like he was falling as Sunlight falls upon a beautiful flower it seeks to open. As a Sun that wants to pour all its light into this one flower and bathe in her colors and perfumes, forgetting that he must also shine for all his people equally. On impulse, he said: 'Marry me, together we can do so much more, be so much more than we can apart; between your beauty and my truth, through our Love, we can bring to birth more incredible goodness than will ever walk upon the Earth.'

"The Queen of Sheba knew there was truth in what he said and replied: 'Yes, I will become your wife and pledge myself to you with this ring.'

"So, for the moment, all was well with the World. Then the Queen asked Solomon if she could see the Temple. Solomon, proud of his achievement, agreed, and the Queen was taken to it as the finishing touches were applied. She was fascinated by the astonishing artistry and marveled at the skill and industry that had gone into it. The outside awakened the beholder to the mysteries of the inner Being. When going inside, all the forms, arches, columns, and vaults led the eye to a sense of infinite space, which spoke of that which was beyond time.

"She turned to Solomon and said: 'I would love to meet the one whose hands and work fashioned all these Earthly elements into such a Heavenly structure.'

"It was like the beginning of an eclipse; a shadow crossed the light of Solomon's mind. He could not explain it, but he did not want her to meet Hiram. He resisted her request but eventually relented. Solomon had fallen into Love from his high place of wisdom; now, he was falling a second time into the pit of possessiveness and jealousy, forgetting that Love can possess one but not possess the one that one loves, but rather set them free.

"The Queen of Sheba met Hiram; he looked up from his work and at her face. Then he looked into her eyes, and the light of his eyes illuminated something in her heart, like a treasure hidden deep in the Earth. With his words, Solomon had lifted her mind into expansive vistas of seeing; Hiram stirred her depths with the look of an artist seeing her inner beauty within the Temple of her outer form.

"Under Hiram's gaze, the Queen felt all the elements of her Being melting in the flame that was beginning to glow in the fire that was being kindled in her heart; not just a flower opening to light, but a root that was grounding itself in all the mysteries of Mother Earth, growing out of it as a daughter of the elements, to combine as the purest expression of the primal enigma of woman. For a moment, she could not speak. She said to Solomon as if to deflect the awareness of what was irresistibly growing inside her. 'Can I meet all the workers who helped build the temple?'

"Solomon, who now felt her slipping away, said: 'There are too many of them; it would not be possible to gather them all from their tasks so quickly. Let's return to the gardens.'

"At this, Hiram leaped upon a stone to be better seen. With his right hand described in the air the symbolical Tau, and immediately men hastened from all parts of the work into the presence of their Master; this impressed the Queen more deeply, and she began to regret her promise of marriage to the King, as she now felt Love for Hiram, to come from the very center of the World; Solomon now felt in darkness and sensed another darkness in himself. All his lofty wisdom now seemed empty and vain if they could not hold this woman's Love; what did Hiram have that he did not? He was a great King, renowned for his inspired wisdom, for all his riches, and for his famous gardens.

"Solomon the Wise began to fall from the heights into that which was base and unwise; he plotted to destroy Hiram and the Love growing between him and the Queen. How could he discredit him? He heard that there were three of Hiram's workers who bore a grudge against him, as he had refused to confer upon them the status of Master artisans, as he had claimed they had neither the knowledge nor did they apply themselves enough to work, to earn the status of Master. One was a Syrian mason, another a Phoenician carpenter, and a third a Hebrew miner. This Triangle of darkness, now formed with Solomon a conspiracy, a confederacy of jealousy, and Solomon, who had conceived the Temple of Wisdom in the service of Love, was now engaged in that which would bring about the destruction of truth and destruction of that which would bring about the Creation of Love. The three craftsmen now became three crafty, cunning agents of those invisible powers that would always oppose everything for which the Temple was built.

"One spoke: 'I always thought I deserved to be a Master; I will make him think again about denying me,' another said: 'I feel deeply slighted; may he know the feeling of humiliation I felt. And the third said: 'He has done us a great wrong, and it is right that we should do unto him what he did to us.'

"Now, which was to be the crowning achievement of Hiram's work was the Molten Sea cast in bronze, which was to have adorned the Temple. All the necessary mixtures of ores had been prepared most wonderfully. The Molten Sea was to mirror the Molten Sea of Love that was rising in the heart of the Queen from all the disparate elements of her Being. However, the conspiring workers adulterated the metals of the casting. They added substances that would cause a catastrophic failure, just as distrust and jealousy can cause all relationships to end in failure and disaster. The Molten Sea was an expression of a new union and cooperation of hitherto separated elements to bring about a never-to-experienced harmony between the inestimable heights and the unfathomable depths of the World.

"A young workman discovered the plot to sabotage Hiram's work. He revealed it to Solomon, thinking that Solomon would act against the plotters. Still, Solomon did nothing to prevent it, as his secret jealousy wished to destroy Hiram.

"The day of the casting arrived, and the Queen of Sheba was present. At the critical moment, the casting failed; a crack of thunder rents the air as if the underworld were to erupt and overflow all Nature. It was just as the plotters had hoped, yet they feared what the darkness within them had invoked in outer Nature. The doors that had restrained all the molten metal were forced open. Torrents of liquid fire poured into the vast mold, where the Brazen Sea was to assume its form, but the burning mass overflowed the edges of the mold, endangering all who had come to view the casting; they fled from the advancing river of fire. Calmly and coolly, Hiram tried to arrest the lava-like flow, dousing it with copious amounts of water; the water and the fire mixed in a primal elemental battle, and the water rose as a dense steam. It fell as a boiling rain, spreading panic among the crowd. Feeling shamed by this catastrophe, Hiram sought in a friend the sympathy of a faithful heart. Still, Benoni, who had informed Solomon of the plot, had died trying to avert the catastrophe.

"Hiram withdrew, oppressed with grief. He had heeded not the danger and possibility that this ocean of fire might have speedily engulfed him. He thought of the Queen of Sheba, who had come to admire and congratulate him on his great triumph and had seen nothing but a terrible disaster. Suddenly, in his loneliness, he heard a strange voice coming somewhere from above his highest aspirations and, at the same time, proceeding from a depth deeper than his most profound knowledge. It cried: 'Hiram! Hiram!'

"He looked up and beheld a gigantic figure; the apparition continued.

"'Come, my son, be without fear; the fire will not harm you; cast yourself into the flames.'

"Hiram threw himself into the fires; where others would have found death, he tasted ineffable delights. He could not withdraw from this state as he felt drawn by an irresistible force. He asked who was leading him on this strange journey and where he was being taken. The voice answered. 'Into the center of the Earth, where the will of the World is forged, so that which is heaviest may scale the heights of the boundless expanses of light, where all that is base, may be led from infinite weight to Eternal light into the Kingdom of Great Cain, where the future of human freedom is wrought from the bondage of the fallen elements. They can taste the fruits of the Tree of Knowledge.'

"'Who then am I, and who are you?'

"'I am the father of your fathers; I am the son of Lamech; I am Tubal Cain.'

"Tubal Cain introduced Hiram into the sanctuary of fire. He initiated him into the mysteries of the original and final fires that will consummate all Creation and the secrets of bronze casting. Hiram was led into the presence of the author of his race, Cain. Cain taught Hiram about the suffering he and his descendants had to bear. However, that suffering was the furnace that had tempered their unconquerable will.

"He blessed Hiram: 'Go, my son, the fires of living thought and burning will be with you.'

"Hiram was brought back to the surface of the Earth and passing time, out of place of Eternal Truth.

"Tubal Cain gave Hiram, before he departed, the Hammer with which he had done great things and a Golden Triangle, which he could carry with him as a pendant around his neck.

"Tubal Cain told Hiram: 'Thanks to this Hammer, and the help of the fires that live, you will speedily accomplish the work left unfinished through man's stupidity and ill will.'

"Hiram did not hesitate to test the incredible power of the precious instrument that could set a heartbeat ringing out through all the metals of the World. And the golden dawn saw the mass of bronze cast. The artist felt a golden light rise from his heart into his mind, and the Queen exalted in the light that shone from his eyes. The people came running, and their astonishment overflowed at the secret power that had been revealed, which in one night had repaired everything. Then the Queen, accompanied by her maids, journeyed out of Jerusalem, and there she encountered Hiram, alone and cast in deep thought. The encounter was decisive; they confessed their Love for each other. And then Had Had, who was the messenger of the fire beings for the Queen, seeing Hiram make the sign of the Tau in the air, flew around his head, and settled on his wrist.

"At this, Sarahil, nurse of the Queen, exclaimed: 'The oracle is fulfilled, Had Had recognizes the husband, which the fiery messengers destined for the Queen, whose Love alone she dare accept.'

"They no longer hesitated but mutually pledged their vows and deliberated how the Queen could retract her vows to the King. Hiram was to be the first to quit Jerusalem; the impatience to rejoin him was to elude the vigilance of the King, which she accomplished by withdrawing the ring, wherewith she had plighted her promise to him while he was overcome with wine.

"Later, Solomon hinted to the three artisans, whom Hiram had denied the degree of Master to, that the removal of his rival, for the hand of the Queen, was quite acceptable to him. So, when the Architect came into the Temple, they assailed him. Before his death, however, he had time to throw the Golden Triangle, which he wore around his neck and on which was engraved the Word of the Master, into a deep well.

"At last, Hiram was found and was able to utter a few final words; he said: "Tubal Cain promised me that I shall have a son, who will be the father of many descendants, who will people the Earth, and bring my work the building of the Temple to completion."

"Then he pointed to where the Golden Triangle was to be found. The Golden Triangle was then collected and brought to the Molten Sea with the Hammer. Both were preserved together in the Holy of Holies. The King caused it to be placed on a triangular altar erected in a secret vault built beneath the remotest part of the Temple. The Triangle was further concealed by a cubical stone, on which had been inscribed the Sacred Law: 'Only those who can understand the meaning of the legend of the Temple of Solomon and its Master Builder Hiram, can discover the Golden Triangle ...'"

The Molten or Brazen Sea

According to the Old Testament account, the molten or brazen sea was a round basin cast in bronze by the temple builder Hiram of Tyre (Hiram Abif) for the forecourt of Solomon's temple. The basin rested on a base of twelve bronze oxen.

Explanation: The completion of the building of the Temple was to be crowned by a work in which Hiram Abiff intended to reconcile the tension and hostility between the sons of Cain and Abel. It was the brazen sea, the casting of which was to be made from the seven primary metals (lead, tin, iron, gold, copper, mercury, and silver) and water, the metal of the Earth, mixed in such a way that the finished casting would be completely transparent.

The casting of the brazen sea forms the core of the Temple Legend. It is a symbol of what needs to be achieved by humanity in the future –

and which can already be worked upon by those who lead the way on the ascending developmental path of humanity. It is the harmonic connection between the element of water, representing calm wisdom, and the element of fire, meaning passion and power.

The brazen sea is made from seven metals harmonically united.

Hiram had made all the necessary preparations for the final casting of the brazen sea in the forecourt of the Temple. However, in his jealousy, Solomon instructed three sworn enemies of Hiram to sabotage this final work. These three individuals, who were workmen or apprentices, had been denied the title of master by Hiram due to their incompetence. They mixed certain elements into the flow of the ore, which caused the entire work to go up in flames. Hiram had made all the necessary preparations for the final casting of the brazen sea in the forecourt of the Temple.

However, in his jealousy, Solomon instructed three sworn enemies of Hiram to sabotage this final work. These three individuals, who were workmen or apprentices, had been denied the title of master by Hiram due to their incompetence. They mixed certain elements into the flow of the ore, which caused the entire work to go up in flames. On a symbolic level, these three evil apprentices represent doubt in the truth of wisdom; superstition, as false beliefs about the constitution of the spiritual world; and the illusion of the personal self that makes us experience ourselves as separate from each other and in our selfishness, stops us from embracing each other as representing one humanity.

In his darkest moments of despair, Hiram hears a voice from the interior of the Earth, asking him to throw himself into the flames. As he throws himself in, he does not experience death as others would. Instead, Hiram undergoes his initiation into the secrets of working with metals and the development of human consciousness. He travels to the inner Earth, receiving the hammer (the Tau cross), the Golden Triangle, and the master word.

On his return to the Temple, with the help of the hammer (Tau), he manages to restore the brazen sea, the symbol of harmony through love between wisdom and power.

III. The Rosicrucian Meditation

Ex Deo Nascimur. In Christo morimur. Per Spiritum Sanctum reviviscimus.

Seraphim – Cherubim – Thrones: Spirits of Strength – 'Let there ring forth from the heights that which in the depths is echoed, speaking: Ex Deo nascimur – from God, we have been born.'

Kyriotetes – Dynamis – Exhusiai: Spirits of Light – 'Let there be fired from out of the East that which in the West takes shape, speaking: In Christo morimur – in Christ, death becomes life.'

Archai – Archangeloi – Angeloi: Spirits of Soul – 'Let there be prayed from out of the depths that which, in the heights is heard and answered, speaking: Per Spiritum Sanctum reviviscimus – in the Spirit's Universal thoughts, the Soul awakens.'

Rudolf Steiner: Foundation Stone Meditation

"We arose from the divine: *Ex Deo nascimur.* We should take all suffering upon us willingly and patiently with the thought that we killed Christ; we should devote ourselves to him entirely and die in him: *In Christo morimur.* Then we'll be reborn, reawakened through the Holy Spirit: *Per Spiritum Sanctum reviviscimus*".

We came over from the Moon, where we were still in the lap of the Gods.
We arose from the divine:
Out of the Father, we are born.
Ex Deo nascimur.

We should take all suffering upon us willingly and patiently with the thought that we killed Christ; we should devote ourselves to him entirely and die in him.

We unite ourselves with Christ on earth and die into him.

"In Christ we die," we may say as we look forward through the gate of Death:

In ... morimur.

Then we'll be reborn, reawakened through the Holy Spirit: Per Spiritum Sanctum reviviscimus.

Then, the Holy Spirit will lead us over to the reincarnation of the earth — Jupiter.

"In the Holy Spirit, we shall be reawakened."

Per Spiritum Sanctum reviviscimus.

"We arise from the divine: Ex Deo nascimur. We must accept all suffering willingly and patiently, bearing in mind our role in the crucifixion of Christ; we must fully dedicate ourselves to Him and spiritually die in Him: In Christo morimur. From this death, we are spiritually reborn through the Holy Spirit: Per Spiritum Sanctum reviviscimus." Rudolf Steiner.

This transformative journey encapsulates the spiritual evolution from our origins on the 'Old Moon', where humanity existed in a divine, nascent state, to our current earthly existence. This progression reflects the deep spiritual doctrines of the Rosicrucian tradition, emphasizing the transition from divine origin through human experience to spiritual rebirth.

In the cosmic view, humanity's journey involved a deepening connection with the Earth, symbolized by consuming the fruit from the Tree of Knowledge, leading to a profound transformation marked by both the embodiment of earthly elements and the awakening of spiritual consciousness. This duality of experience — living through Christ on Earth and dying into Him — is crucial for spiritual evolution.

Steiner suggests that this path culminates in a rebirth through the Holy Spirit, which guides humanity towards a future spiritual reincarnation on 'Future Jupiter', marking a new phase in human development. This esoteric understanding differs subtly from the exoteric by omitting direct references to Christ, reflecting a reverent shyness towards the sacred nature of His name.

Steiner's philosophy extends beyond the narrative of personal transformation to encompass a universal struggle against egoism, which Christ's love aims to overcome. This cosmic battle between egoism and altruism is a central theme in human evolution, where Christ's impulse strives to mend the divisiveness and selfishness that have seeped into human relationships.

The journey towards spiritual enlightenment involves overcoming inherent selfishness through Christ's teachings, which emphasize the transformative power of acts of love and selflessness. This path leads humanity through a cycle of death and rebirth, where spiritual knowledge gained through Christ allows one to navigate life, death, and the afterlife with a renewed consciousness.

Steiner elucidates that before the Mystery of Golgotha, humans had a more direct connection to their spiritual origins, which has been obscured over time by increasing materialism and egoism. However, the Christ event provided a pivotal turning point, re-introducing the direct experience of the divine through the embodiment of Christ on Earth.

This profound spiritual narrative underscores the cyclical nature of birth, death, and rebirth in human consciousness and the eternal struggle to reconcile earthly existence with spiritual origins. The

Rosicrucian meditation — Ex Deo nascimur, In Christo morimur, Per Spiritum Sanctum reviviscimus — encapsulates this journey, highlighting the transition from divine origin (Old Moon), through earthly challenges, to a spiritually reborn existence (Future Jupiter). This transformation is both a personal journey and a universal imperative, reflecting the deep esoteric truths at the heart of Steiner's spiritual science.

"The esotericist should not study for themselves, out of curiosity or the like, but must make the most devoted study a duty for the sake of their own development, as well as for the development of humanity and the world. And when, through intensive study, we have recognized our own essence and know, how and by what means it has come into existence, then we attain a sacred feeling about it. This feeling is expressed in the phrase: 'From God we are born - Ex Deo nascimur.'

When we penetrate deeply with profound earnestness into this feeling and let the etheric currents, already mentioned in the exoteric lecture, the etherization of the blood, through which etheric currents stream from the heart to the head, glow and illuminate the brain, and activate the pineal gland, shining forth like flames in which everything personal dissolves, when we feel how we must completely surrender ourselves in the feeling of wanting to sacrifice our own self entirely, as the spirits, as Christ sacrificed himself for the development of the world, then we learn to express this feeling in the phrase: 'In Christ we die - In Christo morimur.'

And then the certainty arises within us that we ascend to the spirit, resurrect in the spirit. 'Per Spiritum Sanctum reviviscimus.'

Ex Deo nascimur. In Christo morimur. Per Spiritum Sanctum reviviscimus. This is the exoteric saying of the Rosicrucian.

When the esotericist utters this saying, they adhere to what expresses that which we designate as Christ; this is the most sacred to them. Not even with words do they want to go so far; they do not speak the word and let only the feeling speak. Then it sounds like this, when the true Rosicrucian student in their deepest meditation utters the saying:

Ex Deo nascimur.

In _____ morimur.

Per Spiritum Sanctum reviviscimus."

Rudolf Steiner

IV. The Legacy of Christ

The Mission of Human Beings on Earth

Christ, the Logos, and creator of worlds, descended from beyond the Zodiac to the Sun, and from the Sun to Earth. Nearly 2000 years ago, He took human form in Jesus, embodying this vessel for three years until His crucifixion at Golgotha. At His death, as His blood spilled from wounds on the cross, His Life Spirit merged with the Earth's aura. Since that pivotal moment, Christ has been inextricably united not only with the Earth but also with the karma of every individual and with humanity collectively.

In choosing to incarnate into a human body, Christ sacrificed His divine powers to facilitate the future spiritual evolution of humanity, becoming fully human. Through His resurrection in a spiritual-physical body, He united with death and triumphantly overcame it on behalf of all humanity.

At the time of the Mystery of Golgotha, human consciousness was becoming increasingly detached from the spiritual world, as materialism deepened its roots. The Earth and the physical bodies of humans risked sclerosis under the pernicious influences of spiritual adversaries: Lucifer, Ahriman, and Asuras. These forces actively work against the Earth and humanity's ascension.

However, Christ's deed, by fusing Himself with the Earth, offers humanity the potential to transform through wisdom and truth, love and beauty, and power and benevolence. This transformative journey is not only crucial for personal spiritualization and redemption but also vital for the spiritual renewal of humanity and the Earth. The Earth is destined to evolve into a spiritual Sun, a process that hinges on the free and conscious relationship individuals forge with Christ.

Experiencing the flow of Christ's light, warmth, and life between the celestial Sun, human hearts, and the Earth enables us to become conduits for these divine energies, linking the Sun and Earth. As our hearts align with the cosmic heart of the Sun, our physical and etheric bodies merge with the Christ-imbued Earth.

We can act as a bridge between the Sun and Earth by aligning our thoughts, feelings, and will with Christ. This profound union can be cultivated through dedicated meditation and a life lived in alignment with spiritual principles.

"When a person begins to wonder who they actually are, how they can feel within themselves, it must gradually become clear to them that they feel like an egoic entity and that everything they experience in terms of joys and sorrows, everything that drives them to action, is arranged around this center and derives its true impulse from there. Separated from other beings, distinct from them, the human being feels this sense of Self within. Yet, precisely through this 'human I,' they can consciously connect with their environment.

Within the physical body, which represents to the outer world what the human being feels inside as a self-contained existence as if they were a separate entity from the environment, it becomes evident that the heart represents the true center. The heart animates the other organs by sending vitalizing blood to the smallest parts of the body.

Just as the 'human I' is the inner center from which all impulses flow out into the environment, revealing the human being's nature, and to which all sensations from the outer world return, being absorbed and processed there, so too does the vitalizing blood flow from the heart throughout the entire body and then return to this center. The heart is an expression of the human I's activity in the physical body.

There are two types of activity - both in the human ego and in the physical heart: sending outwards and receiving and transforming within. Just as the returning blue blood is transformed into red living blood through the respiratory process within the lungs, the human ego's experiences from the environment must pass through the feelings and sensations of the astral body, thus stimulating new activity.

The human heart performs its activity at a specific tempo; there is a brief period, a timeframe, between consecutive heartbeats. Likewise, the 'human I' requires a particular timeframe between the awakening of the impulse to act and the internal processing of the sensations that interact with the ego from the outer world. This tempo will be different for each individual, depending on their disposition and stage of development ...

The 'human I' is meant to redeem the Earth, lifting it with its powers into spiritual realms, fully aware that it could not develop into what it is intended to be without this Earth.

With the event on Golgotha, as the blood flowed from the wounds of the great Redeemer, as the cosmic heart's blood permeated the Earth and its forces poured into its core, the Earth became luminous, radiating light from within. This event also made it possible for every human individual to experience this light within themselves. When the Earth became the body of the great Sun Spirit as He permeated it with His spiritual forces, all beings on Earth were equally endowed with these forces. The seed for the reunification of the Sun and the Earth was sown. The physical body of Jesus of Nazareth served as the medium through which cosmic forces connected with the Earth's aura.

And when the blood flowed from this body on Golgotha, the Earth was again taken up into the Sun's power.

Since then, this Christ force has been radiating from its center into the surrounding space, and from the Sun, the Christ force radiates into the Earth.

Humans can experience this power, this light within themselves as Earthly beings, when they recognize themselves as a part of the Earth, which is permeated by the essence of Christ as its physical body. Then, the white light from their inner being shines forth, just as it emanates from the Earth's center.

People can also experience the Christ force and the Christ light as it approaches from the outside and permeates them with higher life. It surrounds and penetrates them, just as it penetrates the Earth as it radiates in from the Sun. In this state, a person feels spiritually united with this solar power and senses themselves growing together from their hearts with the great cosmic heart. As higher beings living in this spiritual Sun, they recognize their true Self, intimately connected with it, just as they are connected to the Earth as Earthly beings. And just as solar forces illuminate and invigorate the Earth, this higher being permeates and illuminates the Earthly human with its powers.

Within the temple of the human body exists a Holy of Holies. Many people live within this temple without knowing it. Still, those who sense it receive the strength to purify themselves so they may enter this Holy of Holies. Inside is the sacred vessel, prepared throughout epochs of time so that, when the time came, it could contain Christ's blood and Christ's life. When people enter, they find the path to the Most Holy Place in the tremendous Earthly temple. Many live on Earth without knowing of its existence. Still, once people have found their innermost sanctuary, they may enter and discover the Holy Grail. Initially, the vessel will appear to them as if cut from wondrously glittering crystals, forming symbols and letters, until gradually, they begin to sense the sacred content so that it shines for them in golden splendor.

A person ascends into the sanctuary of their own heart in the Mystery center, from which a divine being emerges and connects with the God outside, with the Christ being. It lives in the spiritual light that shines into the vessel and sanctifies it.

Because humans live as dual beings, they can pour spiritual solar power into the Earth and be a link between the Sun and the Earth. Just as from the center of life, the heart, the invigorating blood flows, and spreads through the entire physical organism, even into the bone system, which can be seen as the outer solidification and ossification in the organism in contrast to the lively, ever-active heart, every human individuality must become a channel for the blood flowing from the cosmic center of life, which permeates the solidified Earth with life. The Earth can be thought of as a cosmic bone structure. It would be entirely ossified and dried out if the cosmic heart had not flowed its lifeblood through a human body, thereby revitalizing it.

Once, the great Sun Spirit demonstrated in a human body what each person should reenact within themselves. Through Him, the possibility is given.

To fill oneself with the Christ spirit and recognize oneself as a center living in this spirit, through which the spiritual light, power, and warmth can flow into the Earth, is the mission of each individual and of all humanity. This is how humanity can redeem the Earth and elevate it to spiritual realms." Rudolf Steiner.

The Etherisation of Blood

"Wherever we, as human beings, have striven for knowledge, whether as mystics or realists or in any way at all, the acquisition of self-knowledge has been demanded of us. But as has been repeatedly emphasized on other occasions, self-knowledge is by no means as easy to achieve as many people believe — anthroposophists sometimes among them. The anthroposophist should be constantly aware of the hindrances he will encounter in his efforts. But acquiring self-knowledge is essential to reach a worthy goal in world existence and if our actions are worthy of us as members of humanity.

Let us ask ourselves the question: Why is achieving self-knowledge so tricky? Man is a highly complex being. Suppose we mean to speak genuinely of his inner life, his life of soul. In that case, we shall not begin by considering it as simple and elementary. We shall rather have the patience, perseverance, and will to penetrate more deeply into the marvelous creation of the Divine-Spiritual Powers known to us as Man.

Before we investigate the nature of self-knowledge, two aspects of the life of the human soul may present themselves to us. Just as the magnet has North and South poles, light and darkness are present in the world, so there are two poles in man's life of soul. These two poles become evident when we observe a person in two contrasting situations. Suppose we are watching someone entirely absorbed in contemplating some strikingly beautiful and impressive natural phenomenon. We see how still he is standing, moving neither hand nor foot, never turning his eyes away from the spectacle presented to him, and we are aware that inwardly he is picturing his environment. That is one situation. Another is that a man walks along the street and feels that someone has insulted him. Without thinking, he is roused to anger and vents it by striking the person who insulted him. We are there witnessing a manifestation of forces springing from anger, a manifestation of impulses of will, and it is easy to imagine that if thoughts had preceded the action, no blow need have been struck.

We have now pictured two contrasting situations: in one, there is only ideation, a process in the life of thought from which all conscious will is absent; in the other, there is no thought, no ideation, and immediate expression is given to an impulse of will.

Here, we have examples of the two extremes of human behavior. The first pole is complete surrender to contemplation, to thought, in which the will has no part; the second is the impelling force of will without thought. These facts are revealed simply by observation of external life.

We can go into these things more deeply and come into spheres where we can find our bearings only by summoning the findings of occult investigation to our aid. Here, another polarity confronts us — that of sleeping and waking. From the elementary concepts of Anthroposophy, we know that in waking life, the four members of a man's being — physical body, etheric body, astral body, and ego — are organically and actively interwoven, but that in sleep, the physical and etheric bodies remain in bed, while the astral body and ego are outpoured into the fantastic world bordering on physical existence. These facts could also be approached from a different point of view. We might ask: what is to be said about ideation, contemplation, thinking — and about the will and its impulses on the one hand during waking life and during sleep on the other?

When we penetrate more deeply into this question, it becomes evident that in his present physical existence, man is, in a certain sense, always asleep. There is only a difference between sleep during the night and sleep during the day. We can be convinced purely externally, for we know that we can wake in the occult sense during the day; that is to say, one can become clairvoyant and see into the spiritual world. The physical body in its ordinary state is asleep to what is then and there happening, and we can rightly speak of an awakening of our spiritual senses.

In the night, of course, we are asleep in the usual way. Therefore, ordinary sleep is sleep as regards the outer physical world; daytime consciousness at the present time is sleep as regards the spiritual world.

These facts can be considered in yet another light. On deeper scrutiny, we realize that in the ordinary waking condition of physical life, man has, as a rule, very little power or control over his will and its impulses. The will is very detached from daily life. Only consider how little you do from morning to evening is the outcome of your thinking and personal resolutions. When someone knocks at the door, and you say, "Come in!" that cannot be called a decision of your own thinking and will. Suppose you are hungry and seat yourself at a table. In that case, that cannot be called a decision made by the will because it is occasioned by your circumstances, by the needs of your organism. Try to picture your daily life, and you will find how little the center of your being directly influences the will. Why is this the case? Occultism shows us that in respect of his will, man sleeps by day; that is to say, he is not in the real sense present in his will-impulses at all. We may evolve better concepts and ideas or become more highly moral and cultured individuals. Still, we can do nothing as regards the will. By cultivating better thoughts, we can work indirectly upon the will. Still, as far as life is concerned, we can do nothing directly to it, for in the waking life of the day, our will is influenced only indirectly, namely through sleep.

When we are asleep, we do not think; ideation passes over into a state of sleep. The will, however, awakes, permeates our organism from outside, and invigorates it. We feel strengthened in the morning because what has penetrated our organism is of the nature of will.

That we are not aware of this activity of the will becomes comprehensible when we remember that all conceptual activity ceases when we are asleep. To begin with, therefore, this stimulus shall be given for further contemplation and meditation. The more progress you make in self-knowledge, the more you will find confirmation of the truth of the words that man sleeps in respect of his will when he is awake and sleeps in respect of his conceptual life when he is asleep. The life of will sleeps by day, the life of thought sleeps by night.

Man is unaware that the will does not sleep at night because he only knows how to be awake in his life of thought. The will does not sleep during the night, but it then works as it were in a fiery element, working upon his body to restore what has been used up by day.

Thus, man has two poles: the life of observation and ideation and the impulses of will. Man is related to these two poles in opposite ways. The whole life of the soul moves in various nuances between these two poles, and we shall come nearer to understanding it by bringing this microcosmic life of the soul into relation with the higher worlds.

From what has been said, we have learned that the life of thought and ideation is one of the poles of man's life of soul. This life of thought is something that seems unreal to materialistically minded people. Do we not often hear it said: "Oh, ideas and thoughts are only ideas and thoughts!" This implies that if someone has [a piece] of bread or meat in his hand, it is a reality because it can be eaten, but a thought is only a thought; it is not a reality. Why is this said? It is because what man calls his thoughts are related to what thoughts really are, as a shadow-image is to the actual thing. The shadow-image of a flower points you to the flower itself, to the reality. So, it is with thoughts. Human thinking is the shadowing forth of ideas and beings belonging to a higher world, the world we call the Astral plane. And you represent thinking rightly to yourself when you picture the human head thus — it is not absolutely correct but simply diagrammatic. In the head are thoughts, but these thoughts must be portrayed as living beings on the Astral plane. Beings of the most varied kinds are at work there in the form of teeming concepts and activities that cast their shadow images on men, and these processes are reflected in the human head as thinking.

As well as the life of thought in the human soul, there is also the life of feeling. Feelings fall into two categories: those of pleasure and sympathy and those of displeasure and antipathy. Benevolent deeds arouse the former; evil, malevolent deeds arouse antipathy. Here, there is something more than and different from the mere formation of concepts. We form concepts of things irrespectively of any other factor. But our soul only experiences sympathy or antipathy regarding what is beautiful and excellent or ugly and evil. Just as everything that takes place in man in the form of thoughts points to the Astral plane, everything connected with sympathy or antipathy points to the realm we call Lower Devachan. Processes in the Heavenly World, or Devachan, are projected, mainly into our breast, as feelings of sympathy or antipathy for what is beautiful or ugly, for what is good or evil. So that in our feelings for the moral-aesthetic element, we bear shadow-reflections of the Heavenly World or Lower Devachan within our souls.

There is still a third province in the life of the human soul, which must be strictly distinguished from the mere preference for good deeds. There is a difference between standing by and taking pleasure in witnessing some kind deed, setting the will in action, and performing such deeds. I will call pleasure in good deeds or displeasure in evil deeds the aesthetic element against the moral element that compels a man to perform some good deed. The moral element is higher than the purely aesthetic; pleasure or displeasure is lower than the will to

124

do something good or bad. In so far as our soul feels constrained to express moral impulses, these impulses are the shadow images of Higher Devachan, the Higher Heavenly World.

It is easy to picture these three stages of activity of the human soul — the purely intellectual (thoughts, concepts), the aesthetic (pleasure or displeasure), and the moral (revealed in impulses to good or bad deeds) — as microcosmic images of the three realms which in the Macrocosm, the great Universe, lie one above the other. The Astral world is reflected in the world of thought; the Devachanic world is reflected in the aesthetic sphere of pleasure and displeasure; and the Higher Devachanic world is reflected as morality.

- Thoughts: Shadow-images of Beings of the Astral Plane (Waking)

- Sympathy and Antipathy: Shadow-images of Beings of Lower Devachan (Dreaming)

- Moral Impulses: Shadow-images of Beings of Higher Devachan (Sleeping)

Let's connect this with what was said previously concerning the two poles of the soul-life. In that case, we shall take the pole of intellect to be that which dominates the waking life, the life in which man is mentally awake. During the day, he is awake in respect of his intellect; during sleep, he is awake in respect of his will. It is because, at night, he is asleep in respect of intellect and unaware of what is happening with his will. The truth is that moral principles and moral impulses work indirectly into the will. Man needs the life of sleep so that the moral impulses he takes into himself through the life of thought can become active and effective. In his ordinary life today, man can accomplish what is right only on the plane of intellect; he is less able to accomplish anything on the moral plane, for there, he depends on the help from the Macrocosm.

What is already within us can bring about the further development of intellectuality, but the Gods must come to our aid if we are to acquire greater moral strength. We go to sleep so that we may plunge into the Divine Will where the intellect does not intervene and where Divine Forces transform into the power of will the moral principles we accept, where they instill into our will that which we could otherwise receive only into our thoughts.

Between these two poles, that of the will, which wakes by night, and of the intellect, which is awake by day, lies the sphere of aesthetic appreciation, which is continuously present in man. During the day, man is not fully awake. At least, only the most prosaic, pedantic individuals are always fully awake in waking life. We must always be able to dream a little, even by day when we are awake; we must give ourselves up to the enjoyment of art, poetry, or some other activity that is not concerned wholly with crass reality. Those who can give themselves up in this way form a connection with something that can enliven and invigorate the whole of existence. To give oneself up to such imaginings is like a dream making its way into waking life. Into the life of sleep, you know well that dreams enter; in the usual sense, dreams which permeate sleep-consciousness. Humans also need to dream by day if they do not wish to lead an arid, empty, unhealthy waking life. Dreaming takes place during sleep at night in any case, and no proof of this is required. Midway between the two poles of nightdreaming and daydreaming is the condition that can come to expression in fantasy.

So here again, there is a threefold life of the soul. The intellectual element in which we are really awake brings us shadow images of the Astral Plane when, by day, we give ourselves up to a thought —

wherein the most fruitful ideas for daily life and great inventions originate. Then, during sleep, when we dream, these dreams play into our life of sleep, and shadow images from Lower Devachan are reflected in us. And when we work actively during sleep, impressing morality into our will — we cannot be aware of this actual process, but certainly we can of its effects — when we can imbue our life of thoughts during the night with the influence of Divine Spiritual Powers, then the impulses we receive are reflections from Higher Devachan, the Higher Heavenly World. These reflections are the moral impulses and feelings that are active within us and lead to the recognition that human life is vindicated only when we place our thoughts at the service of the good and the beautiful when we allow the very heart's blood of Divine Spiritual life to stream through our intellectual activities, permeating them with moral impulses.

The life of the human soul, as presented here, first from external, exoteric observation and then from observation of a more mystical character, is revealed by the deeper (occult) investigation. The processes described in their more external aspect can also be perceived in man through clairvoyance. When a man stands in front of us today in his waking state, and we observe him with the eye of clairvoyance, certain rays of light are seen streaming continually from the heart towards the head. Within the head, these rays play around the organ known in anatomy as the pineal gland. This streaming arises because human blood, a physical substance, perpetually resolves itself into etheric substance. In the region of the heart, there is a continual transformation of the blood into this delicate etheric substance, which streams upwards towards the head and glimmers around the pineal gland. This process — the etherization of the blood — can always be perceived in the human being during his waking life.

The occult observer can see continual streaming from outside into the brain and in the reverse direction, from the brain to the heart. Now, these streams, which in sleeping man come from outside, from cosmic space, from the Macrocosm, and flow into the inner constitution of the physical body and etheric bodies lying in bed, reveal something remarkable when investigated. These rays vary significantly in different individuals. Sleeping human beings differ very drastically from one another. If those who are a little vain only knew how badly they betray themselves to occult observation when they go to sleep during public gatherings, they would try their best not to let this happen!

Moral qualities are revealed distinctly in the particular coloring of the streams that flow into human beings during sleep; in an individual of lower ethical principles, the streams differ from what is observable in an individual of noble principles. Endeavors to dissemble are useless. In the face of the higher Cosmic Powers, no dissembling is possible. In the case of a man with only a slight inclination towards moral principles, the rays streaming into him are a brownish red — various shades tending toward brownish red. In a man of high moral ideals, the rays are lilac violet.

When waking or going off to sleep, a struggle occurs in the pineal gland's region between what streams down from above and upward from below. When a man is awake, the intellectual element streams upwards from below in light currents, and what is of moral-aesthetic nature streams downwards from above.

These two currents meet at the moment of waking or going off to sleep. In the man of low morality, a violent struggle between the two streams occurs in the pineal gland region. In the man of high morality, there is around the pineal gland as if it were a little sea of light. Moral nobility is revealed when a calm glow surrounds the pineal gland at these moments. In this way, a man's moral disposition is reflected in him, and this calm glow of light often extends as far as the heart. Two streams can, therefore, be perceived in man — the one Macrocosmic, the other Microcosmic.

To estimate the significance of how these two streams meet in man is possible only by considering, on the one hand, what was said previously in a more external way about the life of the soul and how this life reveals the threefold polarity of the intellectual, the aesthetic and the moral elements that stream downwards from above, from the brain toward the heart; and if, on the other hand, we grasp the significance of what was said about turning our attention to the corresponding phenomenon in the Macrocosm. This corresponding phenomenon can be described today as the result of the most scrupulously careful occult investigation of recent years undertaken by individuals among genuine Rosicrucians. These investigations have shown that something similar to what has been described in connection with the Microcosm also occurs in the Macrocosm. You will understand this more fully as time goes on.

Just as in the region of the human heart, the blood is continually being transformed into etheric substance; a similar process takes place in the Macrocosm. We understand this when we turn our minds to the Mystery of Golgotha — to the moment when the blood flowed from the wounds of Jesus Christ.

This blood must not be regarded simply as a chemical substance. Still, because of all that has been said concerning the nature of Jesus of Nazareth, it must be recognized as something altogether unique. When it flowed from His wounds, a substance was imparted to our Earth, which, in uniting with it, constituted an Event of the most tremendous possible significance for all future ages of the Earth's evolution — and it could take place only once. What came of this blood in the ages that followed? nothing different from what otherwise takes place in the heart of man. In the course of Earth's evolution, this blood passes through a process of "etherization." And just as our human blood streams upwards from the heart as ether, so since the Mystery of Golgotha, the etherized blood of Christ Jesus has been present in the ether of the Earth. The blood permeates the etheric body of the Earth — now transformed — which flowed on Golgotha. This is supremely important. If what has thus come to pass through Christ Jesus had not occurred, man's condition on the Earth could only have been as previously described. But since the Mystery of Golgotha, it has always been possible for the etheric blood of Christ to flow together with the streaming from below upward, from heart to head.

Because the etherized blood of Jesus of Nazareth is present in the etheric body of the Earth, it accompanies the etherized human blood streaming upwards from the heart to the brain so that not only those streams of which I spoke earlier meet in man, but the human bloodstream unites with the bloodstream of Christ Jesus. However, a union of these two streams can come about only if a person can adequately understand what is contained in the Christ Impulse. Otherwise, there can be no union; the two streams then mutually repel each other and thrust each other away.

Understanding must be acquired in a form suitable for every epoch of Earth's evolution. At the time when Christ Jesus lived on Earth, preceding events were rightly understood by those who came to His forerunner, John, and were baptized by him according to the rite described in the Gospels. They received baptism so that their sin, that is to say, the karma of their previous lives — karma which had come to an end — might be changed and so that they might realize that the most powerful Impulse in Earth's evolution was about to descend into a physical body. But the evolution of humanity progresses, and in our present age, what matters is that people should recognize the need for the knowledge contained in Spiritual Science and be able to fire the streams flowing from heart to brain that this knowledge can be understood ..."

"They are the ether-world condensed; they are the densified forces of the etheric world! Now, from the moment these forces reached the degree of density manifested today by the physical heart, the blood, and the whole circulatory system, they would have come to an end as far as Earth's evolution is concerned, and a kind of death would have set in. The essential and mysterious feature of Earth evolution is not only that this densification took place, not only that the forces that had come over from Old Saturn, Old Sun, and Old Moon condensed to such an organic system, not only that what was in the etheric body became physical, but that as regards each of our systems of organs in Earth evolution an impulse entered whereby what was once etheric and had become physical, is once more dissolved, is changed back again into the ether.

This is so that after the etheric forces have condensed to a system of organs, they are not allowed to rest at this as their goal, but that other forces then intervene, which dissolve them again, is one of the most meaningful impulses of our Earth evolution.

In the very moment when our human organs have reached the point of greatest densification in earthly evolution, certain macrocosmic powers re-dissolve the substantiality of the organic system so that what was there before and had gradually lapsed into this organic condition now emerges from it again becomes visible.

This process can be most closely followed by the occultist in the case of the heart and the blood streaming through it; it is possible to see how this dissolution comes about, how the Earth impulses enter into the substance of such an organic system.

For clairvoyant sight, something streams continuously out of our heart — our heart, the outcome of our blood circulation. If you see clairvoyantly the blood pulsating through the human body, then you also see how this blood becomes rarefied again in the heart, how in its finest elements—not in its course, but in its finer parts — it is dissolved and returns to the etheric form. Just as blood has gradually formed in the ether, we have the reverse process in the human body of the present day. The blood becomes etherized, and streams of ether flow continuously from the heart towards the head so that we see the etheric body built up in the opposite direction through the blood. Thus, what crystallized out from the etheric during the early part of Lemuria to form the human blood circulation and the heart we now see returning to the etheric form and streaming in the human etheric body towards the brain.

And unless these streams of ether were to flow continuously from the heart towards the head, however much we tried to think about the world and know about it, we should be quite unable to use our brain as the instrument for thought. As an instrument for knowledge, the brain would be utterly useless if it were only to function as the physical brain. We must resort to spiritual science to learn how the brain would work today if it were left to itself. The human being would only be able to think thoughts connected with the inner needs of his body. For example, he could think, 'Now I am hungry, now I am thirsty, now I will satisfy this or that instinct.' If he were entirely dependent upon his physical brain, man would only be able to think thoughts connected with his own bodily needs, and he would be the perfect egoist.

But currents of a fine etheric substance come from the heart and stream continuously through the brain. These etheric currents are indirectly related to a delicate and essential part of the human brain called the pineal gland. They constantly leave the pineal gland, which becomes luminous, and its movements as a physical brain organ respond in harmony with these etheric currents emanating from the heart. These etheric currents are brought again into connection with the physical brain and give it the impression that enables us to know, in addition to egotistic knowledge, something of the outside world, something that is not ourselves. Thus, our etherized blood acts on our brain through the pineal gland.

In previous lectures, you will find an even more detailed description of this from a particular standpoint.

There, I pointed out from another aspect something of the function of the pineal gland. So, you see, we have a process within the Earth that leads to solidification and a reverse process of rarefaction. When we grasp this, we are driven to the conclusion that we bear forces that will cause us to revert to the form we had during the Saturn, Sun, and Moon evolutions.

In his ordinary consciousness today, man knows nothing of the marvelous play of forces in his ether body; he knows nothing of this communication between heart and brain. Anyone who is made aware of it through occult development becomes aware of something peculiar about these etheric currents, and here, self-knowledge yields something very striking, something of the highest significance.

One comes to know how these forces stream upwards from the heart to the brain to form the brain so that the human being may be able to use it as the instrument of his soul-life. But at the same time, one learns that these forces have not passed through the human organization unscathed, that they do not leave the heart in the same state in which they entered it. All that man has meanwhile developed out of the unconscious by way of lower instincts and appetites, all his natural propensities, are carried along in the etheric stream, which is borne upwards from the heart.

Thus, we received this current in ancient Lemuria as a pure etheric stream that had no other craving, no other will, so to say, than to condense to form the wondrous structure of our heart. Since then, we have lived as physical men with this heart and this blood circulation; we have passed through several incarnations without knowing anything of this solidification of our original ether bodies into the physical parts of heart and blood circulation. And we have become permeated with desires, longings, sympathies and antipathies, emotions and passions, habits and mistakes, and the reborn ether body which now streams upwards to the brain is darkened, is filled with all this. We send all this upwards from our hearts, and now, in genuine self-knowledge, we become aware of it. We become aware that what we received from the gods in the depths of our life-body we cannot give back to the gods again in the same state in which we received it, but that it has become sullied by our own being."

"This thought, that one is connected with Christ through a spiritual tie, just like a relative is tied to his forefathers through a blood tie, this thought is not a foundation for a Mysticism of Christianity, but rather it is a Christianity that we can denote as a Mystical Fact.

What happened in Palestine some two thousand years ago is a fact that can only be understood through mysticism. Just like the blood relations through generations and heredity can be understood through natural science, the nature of the Christ Impulse can only be understood through spiritual science or the wisdom of mysticism. Through supersensory research, we can understand that the spiritual blood of Christ Jesus flows into the souls of those who find the way to him.

Christ can, therefore, state, even though he was only incarnated once, and looking at those into whom his spiritual blood can now flow: 'I am with you all days until the end of Earth cycles."

"... I have already explained to you that

- Man's glandular processes are an expression of the etheric body.

- his nervous processes an expression of the astral body and

- the blood is an expression of the Ego.

I have shown you that if Christ had not appeared, [then] the development of the blood would have led to a greater form of egoism; the Ego would have increased man's selfishness and egoism more and more.

The unnecessary blood, man's excess blood, had to flow out and be sacrificed so humanity might not wholly lose itself in selfishness. The true mystic sees in the blood that flowed out of the Savior's wounds the surplus blood that had to flow out so that a soul-spiritual brother love might take hold of humanity.

This is how the spiritual scientist looks upon the blood that streamed down from the Cross. This blood had to be taken away from humanity so that man might rise above material things. The love linked by blood ties was replaced by a love that would fully develop in the future, by a love going from one human being to another.

Only in this light is it possible to understand the words of Christ Jesus: 'He who forsakes not father, mother, brother, sister, wife and child, cannot become my disciple.'"

"Then Christ-Jesus came and said to his nearest, most intimate initiates: Hitherto, humanity has judged only according to the flesh, according to blood-relationship. Through this blood relationship, men have been conscious of reposing within a higher invisible union. There is a still higher spiritual relationship that reaches beyond the blood-tie. You can acknowledge a spiritual Father substance in which the "I" is rooted and more spiritual than the substance that binds the Jewish people together as a group soul. See within yourself and every human being in what is not only one with Abraham but one with the very divine foundation of the world. Therefore, Christ-Jesus, according to the Gospel of St. John, emphasizes the words: "Before Father Abraham was, was the I AM!" My primal I mounts not only to the Father-Principle that reaches back to Abraham, but my I is one with all that pulses through the entire cosmos; to this, my spiritual nature soars aloft. I and the Father are one!

These are essential words that one should experience; then, one will feel the forward bound made by humankind, a bound which advanced human evolution further as a consequence of that impulse given by the advent of Christ. The Christ was the mighty quickener of the "I AM."

Now, let us try to hear a little of what His most intimate initiates said and how they expressed what had been revealed to them. They said: Heretofore, no individual physical human being has ever existed to whom this name of "I AM" could be applied; He was the first to bring the "I AM" in its full significance to the world. Therefore, they named Christ Jesus the "I AM." That was the name in which the closest initiates felt united, the name which they understood, "I AM." In this way, we must delve deeply into the most significant chapters of the Gospel of St. John. If we take that chapter where we find the words "I am the Light of the world," we must interpret them literally."

"In Man, the red blood flows as a carrier of sufferings and passions; in the plant, the chaste green juice moves, the Chlorophyll knows no suffering. Just live this thought. Imagine the ideal for humanity's future, when Man will have worked on himself so his blood will become as pure and chaste as the plant's juice. As a symbol of this transformation, we can use the rose green below and transform it into a read above without compromising purity or chastity...

All suffering must be overcome, and the red blood has to become pure again. The Rosicrucian symbol shows the black cross of death and the seven roses as signs of the higher being and becoming.

... in Jesus, the blood again became so pure that after a legend, when the blood was flowing from the five wounds, bees landed on the side of the wounds to suck the blood because it had become so pure that honey could be made from it, just like from the pure blossoms of the plant."

"Hate is the most extreme expression of the I. And where can the I be found? In the blood. Even our physical blood changes when this gate, this hardening process of the I, becoming wooden, is transformed into love. If chemists only had sufficiently fine instruments, they could detect the difference in the blood of an ancient Indian and a Francis of Assisi. This spiritualization is expressed even in the physical. In the blood that flowed for humankind at Golgotha, we have a symbol of 'hate lessness' through which we can transform every feeling of hate into love."

"... the part played by the blood in the physical body of Christ Jesus. The blood is one of the body's physical components. In the case of an ordinary human being, it dissolves away at death in the physical Elements. This did not happen to that part of the blood in the body of Christ Jesus, which flowed from the wounds on Golgotha. This blood was 'etherized' and was actually taken up into the etheric forces of the Earth. The blood that flowed from the wounds on Golgotha became ether-substance. And perceiving this ether-substance gleaming and glistening in the ether-body after death, man knows it to be the young, fertile life by which he is borne onwards into the future.

These quickening, freshening life forces pour into the human ether-body from yet another source. Contemplation of the Fifth Gospel reveals that after the body of Christ Jesus had been laid in the Grave, a certain happening led, in fact, to the scene described with such marvelous exactitude in the Gospel of St. John: the clothes lay scattered around the empty Grave. The Fifth Gospel reveals that it was indeed so: an undulating earthquake had produced a rift in the Earth, and the body of Christ Jesus fell into this rift. The rift then closed again, and as described in St. John's Gospel, the clothes in which the body had been shrouded were hurled about the empty tomb by the storm. These revelations from the Fifth Gospel are a profoundly moving experience when we find them also confirmed in the Gospel of St. John.

What had been received into the rift in the Earth poured through the blood now agleam in the ether, making this gleaming blood visible in the human ether-body.

The ether-body expands after death, and man sees it as a 'firmament' against which everything else stands out in relief. And the feeling arises: The body of Christ Jesus, empty of blood, spreads through the expanding ether-body like a primary substance.

The body that had fallen into the chasm passed into the Earth, and the etherized blood now reveals itself in the tableau of the human ether-body, filling the tableau with life. And from this revelation arises the certainty: Mankind does not perish but lives on as the spiritual essence of Earth-existence when the Earth falls away, just as the corpse falls away from the indwelling spiritual being on man. True, the 'I' and astral body guarantee freedom and immortality for man, but he would live on only for himself; he would pass over to Future Jupiter only to find himself in an alien world if the forces poured by the Christ Impulse into the Earth-sphere were not carried over to Future Jupiter.

138

If individual human beings were not rooted within an Earth-sphere that the Christ Impulse has pervaded, they would pass over to Future Jupiter in 'poverty of soul,' with faculties hardly richer than those belonging to the Lemurian epoch. And this 'poverty of soul', which would give the conviction that earthly life is doomed to perish, would betoken a state of unblessedness for humans between death and rebirth. In contrast, the realization of what the Christ Impulse has wrought for the spiritual part of the Earth brings blessedness to the soul in the life between death and rebirth.

Since the Mystery of Golgotha, every experience by which the human soul is quickened and enriched comes from what was poured into the spiritual aura of the Earth by the Christ Impulse."

"At the beginning of the sixth epoch, an influence will have developed, not in higher spheres, but in the sphere of the present-day conscious mind; in the fifth epoch, this influence is still in its infancy, but it is nevertheless already developing. It is something that emanates from the musical element. For the fifth epoch, music will be not merely art but the means of expression for things other than the purely artistic. Here is something that points to the influence of a specific principle on the physical plane.

The most significant impulse by those directly initiated in the fifth epoch will, to begin with, be given solely in the sphere of music. What has to flow in is not astral, but it is something of great significance in the mental life of the fifth epoch. It is something that human intelligence will come to recognize as necessary, something which has been called the Kundalini fire. It is a force that still slumbers in man today but will gradually gain more and more importance. Today, it already dramatically impacts what we perceive through the sense of hearing.

During further development in the sixth cultural age of the fifth epoch, the Kundalini fire will significantly influence what lives in the human heart. The human heart will have this fire. At first, this is mere symbolism. Still, Man will then be permeated by a force that will live in his heart so that during the sixth epoch, he will no longer distinguish between his well-being and the well-being of the whole. The Kundalini fire will deeply permeate man! He will follow the principle of love as his innermost nature."

"Human perfection consists in the falling away of the lower soul forces so that only the higher forces remain behind; in the future, man will no longer have the lower forces; he will, for example, no longer have the forces of procreation. Above all, John's soul-power will raise those lower forces to the loving heart. It will send out streams of spiritual love. The heart is the most powerful organ when Christ lives in Man. The lower soul-forces are then raised from the abdominal regions to the heart.

Every initiate experienced this in the Mysteries of the heart. It re-echoed in the words: "My God, my God, how thou hast raised me!"

One of the disciples rested upon Jesus' bosom; he rested upon Jesus' heart. This means that all the lower forces, every form of egoism, will be raised to the heart. At this point, Jesus repeated to his Disciples the words: "Eli, Eli, lama sabathani" — "Now the Son of Man is glorified, and God is glorified in Him!

Afterward, he said: "There is one among you who will betray me." The power of egoism brings this about. But as this power of egoism is the source of treason, this lower soul force will be raised to a higher stage.

John's very power of soul will have brought it about that those powers are then lifted into the loving heart. Rivers of spiritual love will flow from it. When Christ is in us, the heart is the most powerful organ in us. The lower power of the soul will then have been raised from the lower abdomen to the heart. Every initiate experienced this as the mystery of the heart. It came to expression in the words `my God, my God, how you have raised me high!"

"People are not ready to form any idea of their reciprocal relation to the very realm of life wherein the Christ is to be found. The influence of the Christ Impulse is not very noticeable in the concept-forming activity of our heads. As soon, however, as we look down into the unconscious, as soon as we turn our gaze downwards into the sphere of feeling and the sphere of will, then we live, first of all, in the sphere of elemental beings. Still, this sphere is interwoven for us with the Christ Impulse.

By way of our rhythmic system — that is, by way of our feelings — we dive into the realm with which Christ has united Himself.

There we come to the place where the Christ is true to be found, quite objectively, not merely through tradition or subjective mysticism."

"Just as Man today radiates the spoken word, one day Man will radiate and express his whole inner being, and it will be impossible for Man to separate his well-being from that of others. Just as the word currently radiates manas, Budhi will be cast through the heart and comprise it directly. Those who have not reached this evolutionary goal will be savages, as this is the normal development.

Today, it is still possible to hurt and wound with the spoken word; this will be impossible with the breath of the heart. We have to transform the word so it cannot harm anymore, as is also said in Light on the Path: 'Before the voice can speak in the presence of the Masters, it must have lost the power to wound.' This is because the not-wounding word retreats to its inner core and develops the heart. ...

.. Regarding the sixth period, the heart has become an organ, and this inner force will pour itself out and urge the heart outwards. In the sixth period, everything goes outwards, and Man becomes wholly heart; the world is his outer body. Man becomes a 'soundwave'; the heart's blood has spread outwards, and the Tone will sprout the inner Meaning. In the sixth period, the outer is the word itself, the Tone, and the Inner is Man himself who lives entirely therein."

"It is the organ which stands in intimate connection with the circulation. Now, science believes that the heart is a kind of pump; that is a grotesquely fantastic idea. The feelings of the soul give rise to the movement of the blood; the soul drives the blood, and the heart moves because the blood drives it. Thus, the truth is precisely the opposite of what materialistic science states. Man today, however, cannot guide his heart as he will; when he feels anxiety, it beats faster since the feeling acts on the blood, which quickens the heart's motion. But what Man suffers involuntarily today will later be in his own power at a higher stage of evolution.

Later on, he will drive his blood of his own volition and cause the movement of his heart as he moves the muscles of his hand today. The heart's peculiar structure is a crux, a riddle for modern science. It has diagonally striped fibers, which are otherwise only to be found in voluntary muscles. Why? The heart has not yet reached the end of its evolution, but it is an organ of the future because it will, in the future, be a voluntary muscle. Thus, it already shows the rudiments of this in its structure. ...

All that goes on in the soul changes the organism. And suppose you now imagine the Man who can create his likeness through the spoken word, whose heart has become a voluntary muscle, who will have altered yet other organs. In that case, you have a conception of the future of the human race in future planetary incarnations of our Earth."

"When a person meditates, this awakens forces in and develops the pituitary gland; it begins to shine brighter and brighter, sends forth rays, and gradually, with its rays, it encompasses the pineal gland lying in front of it and stimulates it. This process organizes the organic formation of the astral body, from the chaos of feelings and sensations into spirit-self or manas. When the pituitary gland causes golden threads to flow around the pineal gland, the time has come when the transformation of the astral body into spirit-self, into manas, has progressed far enough for the etheric body to be transformed into buddhi."

Rudolf Steiner about the Etherisation of the Blood

Christ Sun, Human "I" and the Human Heart

The Sun radiates light, warmth, and life toward Earth and the surrounding planetary system, symbolizing wisdom, love, and power on a spiritual level. The 'Logos'—the 'Word of the World' and the 'Son of God,' the Creator of the World—descended through the cosmos to the Sun Sphere, where He became Christ. This divine entity fully incarnated into the human form of Jesus during the baptism in the Jordan, culminating in a complete merging over the last three years of Jesus' earthly life.

At the crucifixion, during the Mystery of Golgotha, the spiritual essence of Jesus Christ's blood suffused the Earth, merging Christ's solar aura with the Earth's aura. Through His resurrection, Christ redeemed the human physical-spiritual organization from the finality of death. Since then, the forces of Christ embedded within us enable each individual to transform their inherited and culturally shaped personality into a unique individuality. This individuality, forged through the transformative influence of Christ, persists beyond death and into future incarnations.

The descent of the Son of God from beyond the Zodiac through the Sun into earthly incarnation represents the Creator God's ultimate sacrifice to rescue humanity from the clutches of materialism and initiate a new upward evolution.

Through the principle of "Not me, but the Christ in me," our 'human I' can eventually absorb the entire world into our innermost being, becoming a true beacon of wisdom, truth, love, beauty, power, and goodness. Invoking the Sun Christ to permeate our heart and all bodily tissues aids in transforming our thinking to embody freedom, our feelings to resonate with love, and our will to express benevolence.

The Christ Sun within our "I" empowers us to master our consciousness and life, both internally and externally. While our 'personal I' merely reflects our 'spiritual I' within our body, our 'spiritual I' can become a vessel for the 'World I,' the 'Christ Sun,' the 'I am that I am.' Filled with the Christ Sun, our 'spiritual I' masters and transforms our soul, life forces, and physical body through wisdom, love, and power.

Our 'I am' and the Christ Sun inhabit our hearts and blood, central to developing spiritual freedom and selfless love. Embracing the Christ Sun within our 'I am' leads to a purification and harmonization of our thoughts, feelings, and will. This connection transforms the heart into a voluntary muscle, mastering the flow of blood and life forces.

Meditating on the spiritual Christ Sun unfolding within the heart supports the development of freedom, love, and mastery over life. Connecting with the Christ Sun through meditation allows this divine light to illuminate our understanding and actions, elevating them to sacred acts of service to ourselves and humanity.

V. Meditating and Contemplating with Jehovah and Christ

Jehovah and Christ in Rosicrucianism

In Rosicrucianism, "Jehovah" is interpreted within a broader esoteric framework, encompassing not just a religious deity but also a symbol of divine omnipotence and creative forces in the universe. This interpretation is influenced by Hebrew and Kabbalistic traditions, where "Jehovah" is seen through the lens of Jewish mystical texts like the Kabbalah. These texts discuss the nature of God and the structure of the universe through the Tree of Life, attributing profound esoteric meanings to the various forms of the tetragrammaton.

Rosicrucians may view "Jehovah" as a manifestation of divine law and order within the cosmos, associating the name with specific aspects of God's presence and action in the world, similar to the different sephirot in Kabbalah. The discussion around Jehovah extends into theological and philosophical debates about the nature of God, the creation of the world, and humanity's role in relation to the divine.

For practical applications in rituals or meditative practices, Rosicrucians might use the name "Jehovah" to invoke spiritual energies or align with higher divine aspects. This usage of "Jehovah" forms part of a larger tapestry of symbols and teachings aimed at understanding the universe and achieving spiritual enlightenment, initiation and magic empowerment.

Rosicrucianism, which integrates mystical, philosophical, and religious ideas, sees "Jehovah" not just as a biblical deity but as a cosmic principle that governs the laws of the universe. In this context,

"Jehovah" might represent divine attributes like wisdom, strength, or mercy, emphasized in various mystical traditions that influence Rosicrucian thought.

In alchemical traditions, significant to Rosicrucian practice, "Jehovah" is sometimes associated with the transformation and purification processes, allegorically describing the conversion of base metals into gold, a metaphor for spiritual transformation from base human nature to enlightened spiritual existence.

The use of "Jehovah" carries philosophical and ethical implications, representing ideals of divine justice or the eternal struggle between spiritual enlightenment and material bondage. It serves as a reminder of the moral and ethical standards Rosicrucians strive to uphold. Furthermore, Rosicrucians view the divine, symbolized by names like "Jehovah," as deeply interconnected with nature and the cosmos, fostering a holistic understanding of spirituality that includes personal growth and a harmonious relationship with the natural world.

During meditative practices, the name "Jehovah" is used as a focus for meditation, aiming to connect with the divine essence it represents through visualizations, prayers, or chants centered around God's attributes.

Christ in Rosicrucianism is understood quite differently from traditional Christian interpretations. Often referred to as the Cosmic Christ, similar to the Logos in Gnostic and esoteric traditions, Christ is not only seen as a historical figure but as a universal agent of divine wisdom and the harmonic force in the cosmos.

The concept of the "Inner Christ" or "Christ Within" is emphasized, suggesting that Christ consciousness can be awakened within each individual, reflecting the belief in potential spiritual enlightenment and transformation through personal development and understanding.

Christ is considered one of the great spiritual masters, guiding followers towards enlightenment and deeper esoteric understanding.

Rosicrucian teachings interpret many events in Christ's life symbolically, viewing his crucifixion, resurrection, and ascension as allegories for the spiritual trials, transformations, and ultimate transcendence achievable by human souls. This interpretation integrates elements of mysticism, alchemy, and Hermetic philosophy, presenting Christ as a pivotal figure symbolizing the union and harmony of science, art, and spirituality.

Christ's life stages, such as his baptism, temptation, crucifixion, and resurrection, are interpreted as stages of a path of initiation, symbolizing the journey of spiritual initiation and mastery that each individual can undertake. These stages are seen not just as historical events but as spiritual archetypes guiding the individual's path toward enlightenment.

Overall, Rosicrucianism offers a rich and nuanced perspective on "Jehovah" and Christ, integrating them into a broader goal of spiritual enlightenment, cosmic harmony, and the pursuit of esoteric wisdom, making these figures multi-dimensional symbols with deep layers of spiritual, cosmic, and ethical meaning.

Jehovah and Christ in Anthroposophy

In Anthroposophy, the figure of "Jehovah" takes on a unique and intricate dimension that reflects the broader spiritual and cosmic framework developed by Rudolf Steiner, the founder of Anthroposophy. This spiritual movement, which emerged in the early 20th century, blends elements of Western esoteric traditions including theosophy, Rosicrucianism, and Christian mysticism, with a significant emphasis on spiritual science.

Jehovah is associated with lunar qualities and is considered one of the high-ranking spiritual beings known as the "Spirits of Form," which are responsible for giving form to physical matter. Steiner described Jehovah as a monotheistic god, distinct from the polytheistic gods of antiquity, who was particularly connected to the Hebrew people. He is seen as having a specific mission to shape the evolution of humanity's consciousness through the regulation of rhythms and life forces connected to the Moon.

Jehovah is contrasted with Christ, whom Steiner presents as a solar deity. While Jehovah's influence is connected with the Old Testament and the Hebrew people, imparting laws, and guiding the development of the ego, Christ, as a solar spirit, is linked to universal love and the redemption of all humanity. This distinction highlights a transition from the lunar principles of form and separation to the solar principles of unification and spiritual evolution.

Steiner explains that Jehovah's mission involves working through the Moon to provide a counterbalance to the influences of other cosmic bodies, particularly the Sun and Earth. This involves instilling a sense of individuality and separateness, which was necessary for the development of self-consciousness and moral autonomy in humans.

Jehovah is part of a complex hierarchy of spiritual beings, each playing a role in the cosmic and human development. His contributions are specifically tied to the aspects of law, justice, and individuality, which were crucial for the stages of human development depicted in the Old Testament.

Jehovah, often referred to as Yahweh, is seen as one of the Elohim, a group of spiritual beings in charge of cosmic and human evolution. Steiner described Jehovah as the specific Elohim who had a particular connection with the Hebrew people. He is viewed as having provided a necessary focus on the development of individuality and self-consciousness. Steiner taught that Jehovah's influence was especially pronounced in guiding the evolution of the astral body, a component of human spirituality concerning emotions and impulses.

Jehovah is considered to be a Moon God who was instrumental in the development of the Jewish people, focusing on the formation of laws that would foster a sense of individuality and separation necessary for the evolution of consciousness. Steiner posits that the spiritual forces associated with Jehovah acted from the Moon and were crucial in the development of human intellectual faculties and the capacity for reflection. This influence was particularly geared toward creating a boundary for human consciousness to develop in a way that would later make it receptive to the Christ impulse.

Jehovah's guidance prepared humanity for the transition from clairvoyant forms of perception, common in ancient times, to the clear, rational thought processes that characterize modern consciousness. This was a necessary stage in human evolution to allow for a free and conscious reception of the Christ impulse.

Jehovah is not just seen as a deity of a particular people but as a key player in the evolution of human consciousness. According to Steiner, Jehovah's influences through the Moon helped form the human intellect and emotions as we understand them today. The Moon forces, governed by Jehovah, were instrumental in shaping the earliest stages of human self-awareness and individuality, providing the foundation for later spiritual developments facilitated by other beings.

Steiner often described the transition from ancient group souls to individualized human consciousness. Jehovah plays a pivotal role in helping humans move from a state of collective spiritual experience to one where individual ego-consciousness began to emerge. This was crucial for enabling moral freedom and personal responsibility, cornerstones of Steiner's philosophy.

In anthroposophical medicine and therapeutic practices, Jehovah's influence is associated with regulating life rhythms and forces that relate to growth and health. This ties back to the lunar connections, where the Moon's rhythms are seen as impacting biological and emotional cycles in humans. Understanding these rhythms is key to anthroposophical health practices.

Jehovah's connection to the Hebrew people was significant in shaping the spiritual narratives found in the Hebrew Scriptures. These narratives encapsulate deep truths about humanity's spiritual journey and evolution, encoded in the laws and stories that Jehovah imparted. This connection points to a specific phase in humanity's spiritual education, preparing the way for the New Testament's revelations through Christ.

Jehovah's role extends to maintaining a balance between cosmic forces and earthly existence. This includes mediating between the influences of other celestial bodies and the spiritual development occurring on Earth. His guidance is seen as crucial during times when humanity was more susceptible to external cosmic influences.

Steiner hinted at future stages of spiritual evolution where humanity would transcend the current limitations imposed by the Moon forces (associated with Jehovah) and embrace more direct influences from the Sun (associated with Christ). This is part of a larger eschatological view where humanity gradually progresses towards greater spiritual freedom and consciousness.

Christ, on the other hand, is central to Anthroposophical theology but understood differently from traditional Christian theology. In Anthroposophy, Christ is considered a cosmic being whose earthly incarnation in the person of Jesus of Nazareth marks a pivotal moment in spiritual evolution. This event is seen as a turning point that offered a path for humanity towards spiritual renewal and higher development. Christ's mission is often described as one of balancing and harmonizing the various spiritual influences at work on Earth, including those from different Elohim.

Steiner emphasized the Christ impulse as an essential force for human development, enabling individuals to transcend their egotistic nature and evolve towards freedom and love. This Christ impulse is seen as universally applicable, beyond the confines of any one religion.

Steiner's teachings elaborate that the relationship between Jehovah and Christ in the spiritual evolution of humanity is one of complementarity, where Jehovah's role was preparatory, leading to the fuller revelation through Christ. This includes the transition from Jehovah's guidance through the Mosaic Law to the new guidance through the love and freedom embodied by Christ.

Christ, in Anthroposophy, is seen not just as a historical figure but as a cosmic force that incarnated on Earth to bring about a new phase in human evolution. This phase is characterized by the potential for personal spiritual development leading to an enhanced understanding of freedom and love. Steiner describes Christ as a being who transcends the Earthly distinctions of race, nation, and creed, providing a unifying impulse that can lead humanity toward spiritual awakening and unity.

One of the unique aspects of Steiner's Christology is the distinction between the two Jesus children, which forms the basis of his interpretation of the Christ event. According to Steiner, two children born with distinct spiritual heritages were eventually united into one, whose body then became the vessel for the incarnation of the Christ being during the Baptism in the Jordan. This event symbolizes the descent of the Christ being into earthly existence, marking the beginning of a new epoch in the spiritual history of the world.

The relationship between Jehovah and Christ in Anthroposophy is integral to understanding human spiritual evolution. Jehovah's role is seen as setting the stage for the Christ event. By fostering a sense of law, tribal connection, and individuality, Jehovah prepared humanity to freely choose the path of spiritual development offered through Christ's embodiment of love and sacrifice. Steiner's interpretation suggests that while Jehovah's influence was necessary for a phase of human evolution characterized by law and intellect, Christ's influence initiates a phase of freedom, love, and spiritual awakening.

Steiner also ties these spiritual events to cosmic events, suggesting that such divine interventions have both spiritual and cosmic significance, impacting the evolution of consciousness and the cosmos itself.

This complex interplay between cosmic forces and earthly evolution is central to Anthroposophy, reflecting its holistic view of human development as a microcosm of cosmic evolution.

Sun and Moon in Anthroposophy

In Anthroposophy, Rudolf Steiner presents the Sun as the cosmic source of spiritual light and warmth, essential for life and consciousness, symbolizing higher spiritual truths. The Sun is seen as the seat of the Christ being, aligning Christ with Sun qualities such as clarity, illumination, and universality. Steiner posits Christ as a Sun being whose impulse is to bring universal love and the potential for human spiritual freedom, emphasizing the transformative and enlightening nature of Christ's influence.

The relationship between the Sun and the Moon in Anthroposophy is depicted as a balance of different spiritual forces and evolutionary stages. The Sun symbolizes the direction of future human spiritual evolution—toward freedom, love, and higher knowledge. In contrast, the Moon represents past conditions that have shaped the physical and etheric (life energy) aspects of humanity and the natural world. Steiner explains that human evolution progresses from Moon forces to Sun forces, transitioning from the preservation of past wisdom to embracing new spiritual impulses that promote individual freedom and higher consciousness.

The Moon is associated with earlier stages of human development, having a more formative, reflective, and preserving role. It influences Earth by mediating between cosmic forces and Earthly life, affecting growth, reproduction, and rhythm. The Moon holds imprints of old spiritual wisdom and clairvoyant consciousness prominent in ancient times and is linked with Jehovah, whom Steiner described as a Moon God overseeing aspects of human evolution related to law, order, and intellectual development.

Steiner's detailed insights into the celestial bodies of the Sun and Moon relate them to various spiritual and cosmic principles influencing human evolution and Earth's development. He proposed that these celestial bodies represent different spiritual influences and evolutionary forces:

- The Sun is considered the source of life-giving forces, spiritual illumination, and higher consciousness. Its influence is linked to the evolution toward greater self-awareness, the development of individuality, and freedom. The Sun is closely associated with the Christ impulse, central to humanity's future spiritual evolution, intended to lead humans beyond personal egoism toward a universal, loving, and compassionate consciousness.
- The Moon, conversely, is connected to the formative forces shaping physical and etheric bodies. It embodies the ancient wisdom that governed earlier phases of human development, such as instincts, rhythms, and the subconscious. The Moon's forces are related to memory, tradition, and the preservation of past knowledge, attributed to Jehovah's influence, which

prepared the way for the newer spiritual influences of the Sun or Christ.

Mythological Representations: In various myths, the Sun and Moon are often depicted as deities or spiritual beings with distinct personalities and realms of influence. These narratives serve as allegories for the forces represented by these celestial bodies in Anthroposophy. For instance, Sun gods are typically associated with power, clarity, healing, and vitality, while Moon gods often relate to mystery, intuition, and the cyclic nature of time.

The dynamic interplay between the Sun and the Moon symbolizes the crucial balance between evolving forward into new spiritual consciousness (Sun) and retaining essential elements of past wisdom and foundational structures (Moon). This balance is pivotal in Steiner's vision of harmonious evolution, where new capacities build on the stable bases provided by earlier developments.

Sun and Moon in Rosicrucianism

In Rosicrucianism the relationship between the Sun and the Moon holds profound esoteric significance. Rosicrucians, drawing from a rich tapestry of alchemical, Hermetic, Christian, and Kabbalistic teachings, imbue these celestial bodies with deep symbolic meanings, often relating them to spiritual transformation, the balance of dualistic forces, and the revelation of hidden knowledge.

The Sun in Rosicrucian symbolism often embodies divine light, spiritual enlightenment, and the source of life-giving energy. It represents the masculine principle, the active force, and is associated with gold in alchemical terms—symbolizing higher consciousness and spiritual gold. The Sun is portrayed as a guiding force for spiritual awakening and the pursuit of mystical knowledge.

Conversely, the Moon symbolizes the feminine principle, the passive or receptive force, and is linked with silver in alchemical symbolism. It represents the subconscious, intuition, natural rhythms, and the cycles of birth, death, and rebirth, reflecting the Sun's light as a metaphor for true wisdom being a reflection of divine truth.

In the Rosicrucian context, the dynamic interplay between the Sun and the Moon represents the mystical balance between opposing forces—masculine and feminine, active and passive, light and shadow. This balance is crucial for achieving spiritual wholeness and alchemical transformation. The union of solar and lunar forces is often depicted in alchemical texts as the "chemical wedding," a symbolic representation of the mystic union that leads to the creation of the philosopher's stone, which represents ultimate wisdom and spiritual transcendence.

Rosicrucian teachings delve into the esoteric aspects of solar and lunar influences on human behavior and the spiritual development of the soul, incorporating these celestial dynamics as metaphors for stages of spiritual initiation and progression. These phases and cycles are seen as steps in an initiate's journey toward enlightenment. Furthermore, Rosicrucianism integrates astrological concepts, considering the positions of the Sun and Moon in the zodiac and their aspects to other celestial bodies to interpret spiritual forces and time mystical or ritual activities.

Meditative and ritual practices in Rosicrucianism often invoke solar and lunar energies to harmonize the practitioner with cosmic rhythms, enhancing personal growth and spiritual insight. The Sun and Moon, in this tradition, transcend their roles as mere celestial bodies, embodying rich spiritual symbolism essential for the mystical understanding of the universe and an individual's place within it. This worldview frames everything as interconnected through cosmic forces, guiding the spiritual aspirant towards greater wisdom and unity with the divine.

Steiner, in the context of Anthroposophy, further elaborated that the movements and influences of the Sun and Moon are intertwined not only with astronomical phenomena but also with human destiny and the evolution of consciousness. The Moon's rhythms correspond to life processes on Earth, such as the growth cycles of plants and the reproductive activities of animals, while the Sun influences higher aspects of human development, particularly fostering conditions for spiritual awakening and the development of moral intuition.

Overall, in both Rosicrucianism and Anthroposophy, the Sun and Moon symbolize a dynamic interplay of forces that guide both the spiritual and physical evolution of humanity and the Earth. This perspective integrates celestial phenomena with spiritual development, reflecting a comprehensive vision of a universe where spiritual and material realities are deeply interconnected.

Sun and Moon and the Philosopher's Stone

The relationship between the Sun and the Moon in the context of alchemy, which often intersects with esoteric traditions such as Rosicrucianism, is deeply symbolic, particularly in their connection to the Philosopher's Stone. This legendary alchemical substance, reputed to turn base metals into gold or silver and sometimes believed to grant immortality through the Elixir of Life, epitomizes the pinnacle of material and spiritual transformation.

In the rich tapestry of alchemical symbolism, the Sun and the Moon embody two opposing yet complementary forces:

- The Sun is typically associated with gold and masculinity, representing the active principle. It symbolizes the divine spark and purity—the spiritual gold that alchemists sought, which transcends its literal substance to signify spiritual enlightenment and perfection.

- The Moon, contrastingly, is linked with silver and femininity, embodying the passive principle. It represents intuition and the subconscious, reflecting higher spiritual truths manifested by the Sun. Crucially, the Moon is also connected with the purification and transformation processes vital to alchemical work.

A central endeavor in alchemy is the mystical marriage or coniunctio of the Sun and Moon, essential for creating the Philosopher's Stone. This alchemical union typically unfolds through several stages:

1. Nigredo (Blackening): The initial breakdown of the material (often symbolized by lead) into a chaotic, undifferentiated state, representing a kind of spiritual death or putrefaction.
2. Albedo (Whitening): Following dissolution, this phase involves the purification of substances, often associated with the Moon. It entails cleansing and clarification to prepare the substance to receive the spiritual gold.
3. Rubedo (Reddening): The final phase, dominated by the Sun's influence, heralds the arrival of spiritual gold and the completion of the Great Work. This stage symbolizes the attainment of enlightenment, perfection, or the Philosopher's Stone itself.

The alchemical pursuit of the Sun and Moon is not merely chemical but profoundly spiritual. Alchemists regarded their work as a spiritual act, with the laboratory serving as a place of inner transformation. The Philosopher's Stone thus represents more than a literal goal—it symbolizes the alchemist's transformed self, achieved through the harmonization of dualities such as Sun/Moon, masculine/feminine, and spirit/matter.

This symbolic framework has been adapted and interpreted across various esoteric and philosophical traditions to express the pursuit of ultimate wisdom, harmony, and oneness with the universe. Here, the Sun and Moon act as potent symbols of the transformative journey toward higher states of consciousness, where one integrates and transcends human dualities to achieve spiritual completeness.

The enduring imagery and symbolism of the Sun and Moon in relation to the Philosopher's Stone continue to resonate in modern mystical and psychological contexts, underscoring the profound impact and relevance of these ancient concepts in the quest for understanding and transformation.

Christ and the Philosopher's Stone

In esoteric Christianity and alchemy, Christ is often likened to the Philosopher's Stone, symbolizing the ultimate attainment of spiritual perfection and the transformation of the soul. Here's how Christ is associated with the Philosopher's Stone:

Transformation and Transmutation: Similar to the Philosopher's Stone, which is believed to transmute base metals into gold, Christ is seen as a transformative force that elevates the base human condition to a divinely inspired state. This analogy highlights a parallel between alchemical transformation (material gold) and spiritual transformation (spiritual 'gold' or enlightenment).

Embodiment of Perfection: Alchemists view the Philosopher's Stone as a symbol of ultimate material and spiritual perfection. Similarly, Christ represents spiritual perfection and purity, embodying the virtues and qualities that humans strive to achieve through spiritual growth.

Elixir of Life: The Philosopher's Stone is associated with the Elixir of Life, which grants immortality. In Christian symbolism, Christ offers eternal life through his teachings and the promise of resurrection, paralleling the alchemist's quest for immortality.

Mediatorial Role: Just as the Philosopher's Stone serves as the key to bridging the spiritual and material realms in alchemy, Christ is seen as the mediator between God and humanity, making ultimate spiritual truths accessible to humans.

Alchemical Symbolism in Christianity: Many alchemical texts employ Christian imagery, particularly Christ's crucifixion and resurrection, to veil their teachings:

- **Crucifixion:** Symbolically, this represents the 'killing' or dissolution of one's base aspects in alchemy, necessary for rebirth in a purified form.
- **Resurrection:** This parallels the alchemical coagulation or recombination, where purified elements are reformed to create the Philosopher's Stone, symbolizing the alchemist's rebirth into a new state of being, akin to Christ's resurrection.

These interpretations meld spiritual and physical alchemy, suggesting that the work of transforming metals mirrors the inner, spiritual work necessary to achieve enlightenment or Christ-consciousness. This approach exemplifies how esoteric traditions use concrete metaphors to convey complex spiritual truths, making them more accessible through familiar symbols and narratives.

Jungian Psychology and Individuation: Carl Jung, integrating esoteric and alchemical symbolism into psychology, discussed the process of individuation, likening it to the alchemical pursuit of the Philosopher's Stone. In Jungian terms, individuation is the process of self-realization where the individual integrates various aspects of the psyche. Christ, in this context, symbolizes the Self, representing wholeness and acting as a mediator between conscious and unconscious realms, akin to the Philosopher's Stone's role in achieving psychic wholeness.

Alchemical Concept of the Universal Solvent: The Alkahest, or universal solvent in alchemy, capable of dissolving any other substance, is metaphorically similar to Christ's teachings, which dissolve ego and sin, enabling the purification and redemption of the soul. This dissolution is essential for the transformative rebirth central to both Christian salvation and alchemical transmutation.

Symbolic Death and Rebirth: Both Christ's narrative and the allegorical journey to create the Philosopher's Stone involve crucial themes of death and rebirth. In alchemy, materials must undergo calcination and putrefaction as precursors to their rebirth in a new, pure form. Christ's death and resurrection are the ultimate acts of spiritual renewal, offering believers transcendence over physical and spiritual death.

The Great Work: The creation of the Philosopher's Stone, known as the Magnum Opus or Great Work in alchemy, involves stages of transformation each symbolized by specific processes and colors (nigredo, albedo, citrinitas, rubedo). Christ's life and teachings can guide the soul through a spiritual journey from darkness to enlightenment, paralleling the stages of the Great Work.

The Eucharist: The Eucharist, commemorating Christ's Last Supper, where bread and wine are transformed into spiritual substances, mirrors the alchemical process of transmuting ordinary substances into something profoundly significant, akin to turning base metals into gold.

These connections between Christ and the Philosopher's Stone highlight a common theme across various spiritual, religious, and philosophical traditions: the journey toward enlightenment, perfection, and unity with the divine, achieved through profound transformation and renewal. This rich symbolism deepens the understanding of Christ's role in spiritual traditions and the mystical allure of the Philosopher's Stone.

Ephesian Mysteries: JehOvA – I-O-A and Eve

In the Ephesian Mysteries, initiates witnessed the formation of their spiritual essence from the interaction of sunlight and moonlight. During this process, they heard the mantra "J O A" (I O A), which seemed to emanate and sound from the Sun. This mantra was understood to awaken their core self ("I") and astral body. The sequence in the mantra, "J O," represented their core self and astral body, while the "A" symbolized the nearing of their light-ether body. As the mantra "J O A" resonated within the initiates, they felt a deep connection to their ego, astral body, and ether body. It seemed as though, from the Earth itself, a new sound "eh-v" ascended, merging with the mantra to form "J eh O v A." This combination symbolized the Earth's energies rising and integrating with their spiritual selves. Within this new sound "JehOvA," the initiates experienced a holistic sense of their human existence. They sensed a prelude to their physical bodies, which they would fully assume on Earth, represented by the consonants intertwined with the vowels of "J O A," which stood for the ego, astral body, and etheric body. This profound connection to "JehOvA" allowed the Ephesian initiates to undergo the final phases of their journey from the spiritual realm to earthly life.

The connection between the words Yahweh (Hebrew: יהוה YHWH) and Eve (חוה) is not merely coincidental. Eve, representing the great Earth Mother, is encompassed within Yahweh, symbolizing the culmination of ancient evolutions through Old Saturn, Sun, and Moon phases. These phases laid the foundations for the physical, etheric, and astral bodies of humanity. It was only with the Earth phase that the concept of the "I" or self was introduced, symbolized by the letter Yodh (י) in the name "Yahweh".

The name "Eve" in ancient Hebrew, where vowels are not explicitly articulated, embodies all that has transitioned from the cosmic phases of Saturn, the Sun, and the Moon to the development of the Earth. When you combine this symbol, representing the foundational elements of human existence brought over from these phases, with the symbol for the divine entity who governs the Earth's fate in ancient Hebrew thought, you arrive at a name as valid as any other: "Jeve-Yahweh." This name represents the ruler of the Earth, symbolized by the Moon.

This intertwining of lunar forces and their earthly manifestations forms a profound connection. The remnants of these lunar forces, which are visible to us as the astronomical Moon, have also manifested in the feminine aspect of humanity, carrying over from ancient Hebrew traditions. The association of Yahweh, the Earth Lord, with the Moon, envisioned as the Earth Mother, is encapsulated in the name "Jahve." This name vividly reflects the historical and mystical synergy of the Moon's influence on Earth through its governance and the feminine element of human existence.

I.A.O. – The Esoteric Name of Christ

"I am the Alpha and the Omega," declare the words of Christ, the Logos who fashioned the world. The 'I am' represents our divine spark, the innermost essence—the Christ within us.

Meditating on I.A.O. connects us with Christ and aligns us with the dual processes of descending evolution and ascending involution that encompass humanity, Earth, and the cosmos. The Alpha symbolizes the beginning of this evolution, while the Omega marks the culmination of involution.

'I am' is central to the development of both humanity and the planet. The true 'I am' is Christ within us, the Logos—the creator of the world, born within the human initiate, Jesus. Jesus provided Christ his earthly form during the baptism in the Jordan River in his 30th year. For three years, Christ lived within Jesus, endured death on the cross, and triumphed over mortality with his resurrection in a spiritual-physical body, thus conquering death for every human being. Following his resurrection, Christ bestowed the Holy Spirit upon his disciples.

Having descended from the cosmos through the Sun to Earth, Christ now embodies the spirit of Earth and serves as the Master of Karma and the principal guide of human development. Access to the Father God is only possible through Christ, and enlightenment by the Holy Spirit necessitates a connection to the 'Christ within me.'

Christ embodies the Spirit of Love. He is the core of our being, transforming wisdom and power into loving wisdom (kundalini light) and loving power (kundalini fire). Meditating on I.A.O. facilitates our connection with Christ as the leader of human development.

We must endeavor and prepare ourselves; the blessing emanates from the Holy Trinity.

I.A.O. in Spiritual Traditions and Practice

I.A.O. is a sacred and esoteric mantra found in diverse mystical and spiritual traditions, including Western esotericism, Hermeticism, and specific branches of Gnostic and occult practices. The letters "I," "A," and "O" each hold distinct meanings and are interpreted differently depending on the tradition or context.

In Gnostic and occult practices, I.A.O. serves as a powerful mantra for invoking spiritual illumination and connecting with higher realms. It is frequently employed in rituals and meditation to foster mystical and alchemistic experiences and inner transformation.

I.A.O. in Anthroposophy

Esoteric Roots:

IAO is derived from Gnosticism and Western esotericism, where it is seen as an esoteric name for Christ.

Symbolism of the Sounds:

In anthroposophy, the letters I, A, and O can symbolize different stages of spiritual development:

I (Iota): Represents the self or the ego, the individuality in humans.

A (Alpha): Symbolizes the divine or spiritual beginning, often associated with higher wisdom or the starting point of cosmic evolution.

O (Omega): Represents completion or the culmination of a spiritual process, embodying the ultimate goal of returning to the divine or achieving spiritual wholeness.

Spiritual Practices:

IAO can be involved in meditative and contemplative practices within anthroposophy, serving as a mantra or a focal point for initiating deeper spiritual insights and transformations.

Eurhythmy

In Eurhythmy, an art form that integrates speech and music through movement, the I.A.O. exercise harmonizes the three soul forces of thinking, feeling, and will, promoting balance and spiritual alignment.

Relation to Cosmology and Human Development:

IAO, in the context of anthroposophy, thus serves as a bridge between personal spiritual development and cosmic spiritual truths, embodying the journey from individual awareness to universal enlightenment.

I.A.O. in Rosicrucianism:

Anthroposophy shares deep roots with Rosicrucianism, an esoteric Christian tradition that also utilizes the symbol of IAO. In these traditions, IAO is not just a name but an expression of deep spiritual processes. Steiner, who was influenced by and contributed to Rosicrucian thought, integrated this symbolism to express the transformation of the soul through stages of enlightenment.

Ritual and Ceremony:

In anthroposophical practice, IAO may be used in rituals and ceremonies to invoke spiritual presence of Christ and aid in the transformation of consciousness. These rituals are designed to align the microcosm (human being) with the macrocosm (universe), facilitating a harmonious exchange and evolution of spiritual energies.

Artistic Expression:

Anthroposophy deeply values artistic expression as a means of spiritual exploration and communication. IAO might be explored through various forms of art within the anthroposophical community, including drama, painting, and eurythmy (a form of expressive movement art developed by Steiner). These artistic endeavors aim to manifest spiritual truths in physical form and can be seen as practical applications of the IAO principle.

Historical and Symbolic Background

IAO has ancient origins and is found in various esoteric and religious traditions, including Gnosticism and Hermeticism. Within Rosicrucianism, IAO is adopted as a sacred formula. It reflects the tradition's syncretic blending of Christian mysticism, alchemical practices, and Kabbalistic elements.

Esoteric Interpretation:

I (Iota): Often interpreted as Isis, the Egyptian goddess, who represents nature and the feminine divine principle. In a more abstract sense, it can also symbolize the initial impulse or the divine spark within every creation and thought.

A (Alpha): Seen as Apophis, the serpent of Egyptian mythology, representing opposition, chaos, or transformation. This reflects the necessary process of struggle and conflict in spiritual evolution.

O (Omega): Often linked with Osiris, the Egyptian god of the afterlife and resurrection, symbolizing completion, regeneration, and enlightenment. It represents the ultimate goal of the mystical journey.

Theurgical Practices:

Rosicrucians use IAO in ritualistic contexts and theurgical (divine-working) practices to facilitate personal transformation and to achieve higher states of consciousness. It's used in invocations, meditations, and magical operations as a means of aligning with divine forces.

Philosophical and Cosmological Aspects:

IAO encapsulates the journey of the soul through its fall into matter (Isis), its experience and struggle within the material world (Apophis), and its eventual purification and return to the divine state (Osiris). This triadic structure mirrors many other philosophical systems that describe the path of initiation and enlightenment.

Integration in Rosicrucian Rituals:

In Rosicrucian rituals, IAO may be used to consecrate space, invoke spiritual protection, and channel cosmic energies. The vibration of chanting IAO is believed to have spiritual power, helping to harmonize the participants with universal energies.

Connection with Christian Esotericism:

Rosicrucians often blend their practices with Christian symbolism. In this context, IAO is not just a pagan formula but is seen as deeply connected to the mysteries of Christ and the Holy Trinity, offering a bridge between Christian doctrine and ancient wisdom traditions.

Ritual Use and Magical Significance

Vibrational Chanting: IAO is often chanted as a mantra during Rosicrucian rituals to raise vibrational energy and align the participants with higher spiritual planes. The act of chanting serves to harmonize the energies of the body with cosmic forces, which is crucial for effective magical work and spiritual development.

Initiation Ceremonies:

During initiation ceremonies, IAO may be employed to symbolize the initiate's journey through spiritual awakening. Each letter can represent a stage of initiation—beginning with purification, moving through illumination, and culminating in unification with the divine.

Metaphysical and Alchemical Symbolism

Alchemical Transformation:

In alchemical terms, IAO represents the stages of the alchemical process: calcination (I), dissolution (A), and coagulation (O). Each stage corresponds to a transformational process of the alchemist's soul, guiding them from raw beginnings through challenges to ultimate refinement and enlightenment.

Integration of Opposites:

IAO symbolizes the mystical integration of opposites—combining the spiritual (I and O) with the material or chaotic (A). This reflects the Rosicrucian goal of transcending dualities and achieving a state of spiritual and material balance.

Broader Spiritual Symbolism

Universal Life Cycle: The cycle of IAO also mirrors the universal life cycle—birth, life, and death—emphasizing the continuous nature of existence and the soul's eternal journey. It teaches that every end is merely a new beginning in another form, a core principle in many esoteric teachings.

Cosmic Harmony and Order: IAO is seen as a key to unlocking the understanding of cosmic order. It provides a framework through which Rosicrucians interpret the structure of the universe, the evolution of consciousness, and the path to spiritual enlightenment.

Interfaith and Eclectic Symbolism:

The adaptability of IAO in various religious and esoteric contexts (not just Christian or Egyptian) makes it a particularly potent symbol in Rosicrucian practice, which often embraces an eclectic approach to spirituality. This allows members from diverse spiritual backgrounds to find a common ground in its symbolism.

In Rosicrucian practice, IAO is more than a mantra; it is a comprehensive symbol that encapsulates deep layers of spiritual wisdom and metaphysical truths. It guides practitioners in their mystical pursuits, serving both as a tool for personal transformation and as a bridge to higher spiritual understanding.

I.A.O. and the Philosopher's Stone

The connection between IAO and the Philosopher's Stone in esoteric traditions like Rosicrucianism and alchemy involves deep allegorical symbolism and metaphysical concepts. The Philosopher's Stone itself is a legendary alchemical substance said to be capable of turning base metals into gold and granting immortality through the Elixir of Life. Its significance extends far beyond physical transformation, symbolizing the ultimate achievement of spiritual perfection and enlightenment.

Stages of Alchemical Transformation:

I (Iota) in the context of alchemy, can represent the initial blackening phase of alchemy known as 'nigredo', which is the stage of decomposition or putrefaction where all impurities begin to break down. This stage is essential as it represents a spiritual mortification and the killing of the ego necessary for further purification.

A (Alpha) could be seen as 'albedo', the whitening or purification phase, where the alchemist cleanses the material (and by extension, the soul) of its impurities. This phase is marked by a purification and a clarification of the substance being transformed.

O (Omega) symbolizes 'rubedo', the reddening phase, which is the culmination of the alchemical process. This stage represents the coagulation of the purified substance into the Philosopher's Stone, symbolizing the achievement of enlightened wisdom and the integration of the spiritual with the material.

Alchemy

In alchemical contexts, I.A.O. reflects the transformative stages:

"I" denotes calcination or dissolution, processes that break down the ego and impurities.
"A" implies coagulation or concretion, where purified elements consolidate.
"O" symbolizes sublimation or spiritualization, marking the attainment of higher consciousness.

Hermeticism

Within Hermeticism, I.A.O. embodies the three alchemical principles:

"I" for sulfur (spirit),
"A" for mercury (soul),
"O" for salt (body). These elements are foundational in understanding the nature of reality and the spiritual path.

Spiritual and Cosmic Integration:

The process symbolized by IAO can be likened to the creation of the Philosopher's Stone, which is not merely a physical alchemy but a significant spiritual journey. The transformation from base to noble, from mortal to immortal, reflects the spiritual ascension and evolution towards a divine state.

Mantra and Meditative Focus:

Silentluy chanting IAO in the context of seeking the Philosopher's Stone can be used as a form of meditation to focus the mind and align the spirit with the cosmic and internal processes necessary for this profound transformation. Each iteration of the chant drives deeper spiritual insights and aids in manifesting the internal changes mirrored by the alchemical operations.

Gnostic and Mystical Connections:

Both the Philosopher's Stone and the IAO formula are deeply embedded in Gnostic thought, where material existence is seen as a state to transcend, and spiritual knowledge (gnosis) leads to ultimate salvation and enlightenment. IAO encapsulates this journey from ignorance to gnosis, much like the transformation of base metal into gold symbolizes a move from darkness to divine light.

Conclusion

In essence, the relationship between IAO and the Philosopher's Stone in esoteric traditions represents the comprehensive path of spiritual evolution. It's about the transformation and elevation of the human soul, life and body from a state of base, earthly existence to one of enlightened spiritual existence, akin to the alchemical gold. This process is internal and mystical, and alchemical, physically transformative, and IAO provides the activation of forces with soul, life and body that transform our human nature and the Erath to create the Philosopher's Stone.

From T.A.O. to I.A.O.

In the era of Atlantis, humanity was attuned to the universal spirit of nature through the resonant sound of T.A.O., the Sun's glorious sound. This ancient sound allowed human souls to transcend their physical forms and merge with the Divine spirit of nature. Through T.A.O., individuals could connect with the mirror image of Christ, the great Sun Spirit, before His earthly descent.

The TAU, associated with T.A.O., purified and fortified human will, aligning it with the overarching goals of human evolution. Since Christ's incarnation—His birth, three-year ministry, death, and resurrection—He has become Earth's guiding spirit and the Master of human karma. Christ's deeds have set the stage for Earth's reunion with the spiritual Sun, allowing humanity to pursue freedom, love, and mastery over life across incarnations.

Christ endowed the human "I" with the capacity to transform our lower bodies into a full expression of the divine Trinity, elevating the "I" to its highest potential rather than letting it be extinguished in spiritualization. This transformation was made possible by Christ's death and resurrection, which enabled humans to forge a physical-spiritual resurrection body, maintaining self-awareness beyond death. Our inner, loving connection with Christ facilitates the creation of the Philosopher's Stone.

Christ's life, death, and resurrection have forged a new covenant between humans and God, founded on the development of individual freedom, love, and mastery of life. His teachings, as expressed in the Scriptures, underscore this new relationship:

John 8:32 - "Then you will know the truth, and the truth will set you free."

Matthew 22:36-40 - "Master, which is the great commandment in the law? Jesus said unto him, Thou shalt love the Lord thy God with all thy heart, and with all thy soul, and with all thy mind. This is the first and greatest commandment. And the second is like unto it: Thou shalt love thy neighbor as thyself. On these two commandments hang all the law and the prophets."

These passages epitomize the essence of Christianity inspired by Saint Paul, who argues that the developed human being will pursue the Good not out of fear of divine retribution but because they freely recognize goodness as the objective of humanity's ascending development and thus will embrace it out of love for Christ, ourselves, nature, humanity, and the spirit world.

The I.A.O. mantra encapsulates this vision:

I stands for "I am," the name of Christ, representing our divine essence.

A stands for Alpha, our evolutionary past, embraced with love.

O stands for Omega, our evolutionary future, approached with genuine enthusiasm as we strive toward the development goals of humanity and Earth, empowering our actions.

These elements of I.A.O. also correspond to planetary influences:

I – Mercury, preparing humanity's connection with the Christ Sun.

A – Venus, fostering universal love.

O – Jupiter, inspiring freedom and enthusiasm for truth and human development.

Through meditation and mindful reflection on I.A.O., we align ourselves with Christ's lead, progressing toward the Father and the Holy Spirit through love and freedom, enhancing our spiritual journey and contributing to the cosmic evolution.

I am the Alpha and the Omega

"The goal of this esoteric lesson is always deeper penetration into esotericism until we can pass over into mantric exercises. We must set aside our illusions to push forward to the great secret. At certain stages of evolution, illusions are necessary for human beings. An esoteric pupil will, with time, set them aside.

The grand illusion of the personal "I" must be set aside. The true "I" of the human being is not contained in this illusion but instead comes out of the indefinite and takes its course into the infinite.

Through the senses, we become conscious of the 'I' in the physical world. The etheric head and physical brain united during the Atlantean epoch. As a result, the 'I' entered into the human being. Yet this 'I' was, so to speak, only like a small pocket that sank into the human being.

And the true 'I' is spread out through the planets from Old Saturn to Future Vulcan, radiated into it.

The best symbol is that this little pocket is like a mirror into which the true 'I' streams from this string of planetary stages throughout evolution.

I said it goes indefinitely because it did not begin in Old Saturn. After the Future Vulcan state, it continues further. Therefore, we imagine it as a line on which individual personal lives are formed like running knots.

If we know how to extinguish the personal 'I' that we become conscious of through the senses, then the line that leads from the indefinite into the indefinite lies before us:

"The illusion of the senses covers the illusion of time."

Yet it lies before us as a line only through the illusion of time. If this line is somewhat curved, it must close in a circle.

Therefore, the second sentence:

"The illusion of time separates Alpha Omega."

The I.A.O. and the true 'I' are symbolically expressed in the snake that bites its tail.

The 'I' Alpha Omega = I A O was the foundation for the Atlantean Tau."

"...Moses and Hermes were Zarathustra's disciples. He gave his astral body to Hermes and his etheric body to Moses. Moses was the first to proclaim the teaching that emanated from the Akasha Chronicle, the teaching of the 'I am the I am.' (Ejeh asher ejeh) ...

Regardless of whether you regress or progress, whether you seek God in the Alpha or in the Omega, you will be able to find Him. What is important is that you find Him with your own heightened human power.

Those forces necessary to find the God of the Alpha are the primal forces of a human being. However, the forces necessary to find the God of the Omega must be acquired here on Earth by striving human beings themselves.

Whether one goes back to Alpha or forward to Omega, it makes a difference. He who is content with finding God and wants to get into the spiritual world has the choice of going forward or backward. However, the individual who is concerned that humanity leaves the Earth in a heightened state must point the way to Omega — as did Zarathustra."

"When the human passed over from the Atlantean to the post-Atlantean age, he could not do many of the things he does now. You see, from a certain time of your childhood upward, you can say "I" when referring to yourself. You pronounce the word "I" very carelessly. But during the development of humanity, this word was not always uttered so carelessly. There were older times in the evolution of humanity — though even in ancient Egypt, these olden times had, to a great extent, already waned — there were older times in which the I was designated by a name. If someone uttered this name, it dazed people. People, therefore, avoided pronouncing it.

If the name applicable to the I, which was only known to the initiates, had been pronounced in the presence of people in the times immediately following the Atlantean catastrophe, the sound of this name would have dazed the whole congregation; all the people would have fallen to the ground, so strong would have been the effect of the name applicable to the I.

An echo of this may still be found among the ancient Hebrews, where one spoke of 'the unutterable name of God in the soul,' a name which could only be pronounced by the initiates or shown to the congregation in eurhythmic gestures. Therefore, the origin of God's unutterable name may be seen in the facts explained to you just now.

But little by little, this name was lost. And with it was lost the profound effect which radiates from such things."

Meditation and Contemplation

Sounding the Mantra I.A.O., vocalize each letter separately, prolonging the sound of each vowel.

Pronunciation

I – as in **ea**gle　　A- as in f**a**ther　　O – as in r**o**se

Duration of each sound

Draw out the sounds that each sound has an equally long duration of 1/3 of the inhalation or exhalation and pronounce them as follows:

EEEEEEEEEEEE – AAAAAAAAAAAH – OOOOOOOOOOOO

Contemplation

As part of your Contemplation, remind yourself of what each of the following stands for:

'**I**' – 'I am', the name of the Christ, and our innermost essence and mastery of life. The sound 'I' can help to balance and interweave freedom, and love.

'**A**' – the gift of the Love and Compassion of Christ

'**O**' – the gift of the Wisdom and Truth of Christ

Meditating

'**I**' – 'I am" - connects us with Christ – 'In Christo morimur.'

'**A**' – 'Alpha' – connects us with the Father God – 'Ex Deo nascimur.'

'**O**' – 'Omega' – connects us with the Holy Spirit – 'Per Spiritum Sanctum reviviscimus.'

The "I" in thinking, feeling and willing.

'**I**' – Mercury: "I think"

'**A**' – Venus: "I feel"

'**O**' – Jupiter: "I will"

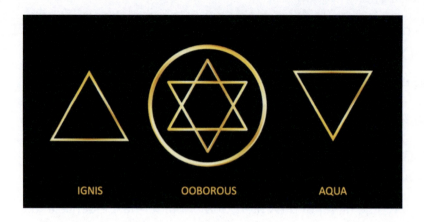

IGNIS   OOBOROUS   AQUA

'I' – Ignis – Fire   'A' – Aqua – Water   'O'– Oobourus

Ex Deo nascimur - From God we are born. (Evolution) - **A**

In Christo morimur - In Christ we die. (Turning point) - **I**

Per Spiritum Sanctum reviviscimus - In the Holy Spirit we are reborn. (Involution) – **O**

I - "I am" – Balance, Harmony, and Rhythm

A – Selfless Love

O – Individual Freedom

In addition to your meditation practice, consider dedicating time to contemplate the deeper meanings and implications of qualities such as **wisdom, truth, love, forgiveness, power, benevolence, and mastery of life**. Reflect on how embodying these virtues could enhance not only your own life but also the lives of those around you, both in personal and professional contexts.

Think about the specific ways in which integrating these virtues can improve your relationships and daily interactions. For instance, consider how adopting a mindset of forgiveness might resolve conflicts more harmoniously, or how practicing benevolence could foster a more supportive and caring environment at work.

By actively contemplating these qualities and feeling genuinely enthusiastic about incorporating them into your life, you can enrich your meditation sessions. This approach doesn't just deepen your practice but also brings a heightened focus and vitality to it, bridging the gap between contemplative practice and practical application.

This thoughtful integration of virtues into everyday life not only makes your meditation practice more meaningful but also amplifies its effects, allowing you to live a life more aligned with these elevated principles.

Meditation

Meditating with Mantras: When you use mantras during meditation, focus on the experience rather than intellectualizing the sounds. Follow these steps to deepen your practice:

1. **Silently speak**: Articulate each mantra clearly without thinking about its meaning.
2. **Feel**: Listen to and embrace the feelings that each sound evokes within you.
3. **Want**: Desire the essence and power that each mantra represents.
4. **Perceive Silence**: Pay attention to the silence between sounds. Allow each word or sound to resonate fully in the brief quiet moments. In the silence between sounds, listen deeply to the reverberations of the mantras
5. **Breathe Evenly**: Maintain a smooth and steady flow of breath, focusing your attention continuously on your heart.

This method helps each mantra to fully manifest its power within your consciousness, enhancing the depth and effectiveness of your meditation.

Developing Individual Freedom and Selfless Love: To foster personal freedom, selfless love and success:

- **Goal Selection**: Choose objectives that resonate with your personal values and aspirations.
- **Goal Contemplation**: Reflect on how achieving these goals will benefit not only yourself but also those around you and the environment.
- **Goal Achievement**: Work diligently towards these goals while ensuring alignment with the needs of your community and the natural world.

To cultivate love and compassion in your interactions:

- **Active Listening**: Engage fully with others, listening without judgment or distraction. This practice fosters deeper understanding and connection.
- **Mindful Nature Observation**: Spend time in nature, observing its beauty and rhythms attentively. This nurtures a sense of kinship and care for the environment.

The love and undivided attention you offer to others and to nature invariably enrich your life, enhancing your appreciation of life and contributing to your happiness. These practices not only benefit you but also ripple out to positively impact those around you.

Some problems you may face

1. **Choosing the Right Time:**
   o Select a time of day when you feel naturally alert to prevent the likelihood of falling asleep. Early morning after waking or evening before bedtime are optimal times.

Morning sessions can energize your day, while evening sessions can help unwind and ensure quality sleep.

2. **Adjusting Your Position**:
   o If you find yourself frequently falling asleep, consider sitting in a less comfortable position, such as upright on a stool without back support. This can help maintain alertness.
   o Conversely, if you are often overly alert or tense, lying down may help in achieving relaxation necessary for effective meditation.

3. **Handling Sleepiness:**
   o It's common to fall asleep during meditation, especially if you are sleep-deprived or exhausted. While this is acceptable initially, strive to stay awake through the session as you practice more.

4. **Dealing with Distractions:**
   o Your mind might wander during meditation, drawn by thoughts, memories, emotions, or sensations. Instead of trying to suppress these distractions, briefly examine what they might signify, acknowledge their presence, then consciously refocus on your meditation.
   o This approach not only helps in managing distractions but also in understanding underlying patterns or issues that may surface during meditation.

5. **Improving Meditation Skills:**
   o Regular practice will enhance your ability to focus, concentrate, and remain alert while also deepening relaxation and the ability to enter meditative trance states.
   o Consistency is key—aim to meditate daily or as regularly as possible to observe improvements.

When should I meditate, and for how long?

   o Practice the Sun Meditation two or better three times daily.
   o Best time: in the morning after waking, before lunch, and in the at bedtime

- o Duration: 20 minutes per meditation session
- o **Be patient!** Learning how to meditate effectively is a skill that requires time.

VI. The Sun and Moon Meditation

Part 1: Rosicrucian Meditation

Practice and maintain heart focus and Coherence Breathing throughout the invocation and evocation of the Holy Trinity.

- Imagine the Jehova Moon and the Christ Sun merging in your heart.
- With each exhalation silently speak the following four mantras below in your heart.
- Perceive silence between the words (breaks), so that each word can reverberate within the silence.
- Maintain the even flow of your breath, whilst continuously focusing on your heart. Listen the words in the silent breaks.

Ex Deo nascimur.

In Christo morimur.

Per Spiritum Sanctum reviviscimus.

I am Alpha and Omega.

Part 2: Merging Sun and Moon in the Heart

Practice and maintain the Coherence Breathing throughout this meditation.
Imagine the Jahve Moon and the Christ Sun merging in your heart.

With each inhalation silently speak **"IehOvA"** in your heart.
("IehOvA")
With each exhalation silently speak "**I.A.O.**" in your heart.
("**I** am **A**lpha and **O**mega")

Perceive silence between each sound, so that each sound can reverberate within the silence. Maintain the even flow of your breath, whilst continuously focusing on your heart. Listen to each sound in the short silent breaks.
(Duration: 15 minutes)

Part 3: I am Power, Love, Wisdom

Imagine Moon and Sun in your heart.
On exhalation silently speak: "**I am Power, Love, Wisdom.**"
('I am' is the name of Christ and referrers to yourself. 'I am' is Christ within you.)

Part 4: Listening into the Silence

For the next 5 minutes maintain focus on the heart and listen into the silence.

Practice the Sun and Moon Meditation two to three times daily.
(After waking, before lunch, at bedtime)

VII. A Path towards Rosicrucian Initiation

Christian Esoteric Development as Service to Humanity

The pathway delineated in this book follows the 'Chymical Wedding,' an esoteric process of union with Christ and the Holy Trinity, assisted by the 'Rosicrucian Meditation' and the 'Sun and Moon Meditation'. This spiritual journey aims at the redemption of nature through the spiritualization of the physical body, crafting the resurrection body of Christ within us, and forging the Philosopher's Stone as we strive towards the creation of a 'New Earth.'

To embark on this path of initiation, one must first engage deeply with the teachings of Rudolf Steiner, especially his reflections on the pivotal role of one's relationship with Christ and the Holy Trinity. This foundational understanding is further enriched through contemplative and meditative engagement with Rosicrucian initiation dramas such as The Chymical Wedding, The Temple Legend, The Golden Age Restored, and The Parabola.

The esoteric development outlined here is intended as a service to humanity, where the cultivation of wisdom and selfless love culminates in sacrificial service. This transformative process often involves painful self-awareness and the conscious processing of past traumas, enabling inner growth and purification of thoughts, feelings, and will. Through these trials, these faculties are refined and aligned with the human 'I', merging with the Holy Trinity and Christ.

Embarking on this path may initially intensify life's challenges. You may encounter growing obstacles and become more aware of personal limitations. However, this awareness encourages taking responsibility for one's destiny and seeking ways to enhance both personal growth and the well-being of others in alignment with the Holy Trinity and Christ.

Occult development can also increase one's influence and power. It is imperative to wield this increased capacity with the utmost integrity, channeling it into societal service rather than personal gain. The path of Rosicrucian initiation is a commitment to Christ—a journey towards wisdom, selfless love, and purposeful sacrifice. It is a slow and gradual transformation, with progress tailored to each individual's pace.

As you navigate this path, you may face significant life challenges and losses, which can instill humility and deepen your understanding of life's transient nature. Overcoming these difficulties, processing grief, and discovering the hidden blessings within these experiences can foster compassion, self-compassion, and a trust in spiritual guidance. Such trials can become profound teachers, echoing Christ's own narrative of death and resurrection.

Christian Rosenkreuz and Rudolf Steiner have emerged as spiritual guides, helping us to evolve as human beings and to contribute meaningfully to the ascending evolution of humanity and Earth.

Steps of this esoteric training programme

Stage 1: Study of Rudolf Steiner's Research about Christ, the Holy Trinity, and the Philosopher's Stone

Stage 2: Contemplate the content of your study (Heart thinking)

Stage 3: Meditate the and Moon Meditation for 20 minutes in the morning and evening.

References

Rudolf Steiner

An Esoteric Cosmology, GA94. Paris, May-June 1906.

Theosophy of the Rosicrucian, GA 99, IVX. The Nature of Initiation. Munich, 6 June 1907.

The Temple Legend. Lecture 9. The Essence and Task of Freemasonry from the Point of View of Spiritual Science. Third lecture. Berlin, 16.12.1904.

An Outline of Occult Science. Chapter V. Knowledge of the Higher Worlds. 1910.

The Working of Natural Substance and Spiritual Essence in the visible World. GA 98. Part I, 3. The Rosicrucian Initiation. Düsseldorf, 15 December 1907.

Esoteric Lessons, Number 9, GA 266, Berlin, 06.06.1906.

Esoteric Lesson, GA 266/1, 16.01.1908.

The Principle of Spiritual Economy, GA 109, VII. The Macrocosmic and the Microcosmic Fire: The Spiritualization of Breath and Blood, Cologne 10.04.1909.

Toward Imagination, GA 169. 3. The Twelve Human Senses. Berlin, 20.06.1916.

Rosicrucianism Renewed. Images of Occult Seals and Pillars. The Munich Congress. Comments on Details of the Arrangement of the Meeting Hall, Lecture 5, GA 284, Munich 21.05.1907.

Commentary on the Arrangement of the Conference Hall. Lecture. Munich, 21 May 1907.

Cosmic being and ego-hood. GA 169. Berlin, 20 June 1916.

The Secret of the Mystery of Golgotha takes place between the heart and the lungs. In Peter Selg: The Mystery of the Heart: Studies on the Sacramental Physiology of the Heart. SteinerBooks, Inc; 2nd edition (20 Mar. 2012).

Collected Essays. GA 35. Die chymische Hochzeit des Christian Rosenkreuz. 1917.

Impulses of Spiritual Science Origin. Berlin, 22.10.06: GA 96.

Sayings, Poems, Mantras. Supplementary volume. GA 40a.

Fourth Part of the Foundation Stone Meditation, GA 260, Dornach 1924.

Esoteric Lessons II, Lesson 26, GA 266, Hannover 05..03.1911

Esoteric Lesson II, Lesson 33, GA 266, Norrkoping, 14.07.1914

Love and its Meaning in the World, GA 143, Zurich,17.12.1912,

The Inner Nature of Man and the Life between Death and New Rebirth. Lecture 4, GA 153.   Vienna 12.04.1914.

Consciousness - Live - Form. Fundamental principles of a spiritual-scientific Cosmology. GA 89. Berlin 1904.

Three Paths to Christ. GA 143. Jan – Dec 1912.

Freemasonry and Ritualistic Work. On the history and contents of the gnostic-cultic Section of the Esoteric School. GA 265. 1904 to 1914.

Soul Exercises with Word and Symbol meditations. GA 267, 1904 – 1924.

Cosmic Forces in Man. GA 209, Oslo 2021.

Esoteric Lessons. GA 266/II.

The Mission of Human Beings on Earth, GA 265, Location, and date unknown.

The Mission of Christian Rosenkreuz. The Etherisation of Blood. The reappearance of Christ in the Etheric. GA 130, 1 October 1911, Basel.

Occult Physiology GA 128.

Wonders of the World, Ordeals of the Soul, Revelations of the Spirit. The true meaning of ordeals of the soul. Progressive gods and backward beings. The Mystery of Golgotha. GA 129. Lecture VIII. GA 129. 25.08.1911.

Wonders of the World, Ordeals of the Soul, Revelations of the Spirit. Eagle, Bull and Lion currents. Sphinx and Dove. Ego-consciousness. GA 129. Lecture IX. GA 129. Munich, 26.08.1911.

Theosophy and Rosicrucianism, GA 100, Lecture XII, The Stages of Christian Initiation, Karlsruhe, 27.09.1927.

The Gospel of St John. GA 103. Lecture III. The Mission of the Earth. Hamburg, 20.05.1908

Introduction into the Foundation of Theosophy. GA 111. 30.03.1909

Esoteric Lessons, GA 266/1. Dusseldorf, 15.04.1909

From Akashic Research: The Fifth Gospel. GA 148. Berlin, 10.02.1914.

The Trojan War. Greek and Mythology in the Light of Esotericism. Lecture IV. GA 92, Berlin, 28.10.1904.

The Mission of Michael. The Revelation of the Intrinsic Secret of the Human Being. GA 194. Lecture VII. Elemental Beings and Human Destinies. Dornach, 06.12.1919.

The Future Rounds, GA 90A, Berlin, 15.06.1904.

Theosophy of the Rosicrucians. GA 99. Lecture XIII. Munich, 05.06.1917.

Esoteric Lesson. GA266/1. Berlin, 07.01.1908.

The Easter Festival in Relation to the Mysteries. GA 233a. Lecture IV. The Mysteries of Ephesus. The Aristotelian Categories. Dornach, 22.04. 1924

Christus and the Spiritual World: The Search ofr the Holy Grail. Lecture IV. GA 149, Leipzig, 02.01.1914.

Esoteric Lessons, GA 266A, Munich 15.06.1908.

Education as a Social Problem. VI. The Inexpressible Name, Spirits of Space and Time, Conquering Egotism. GA 296. Dornach, 17.08.1919.

The Temple Legend and the Golden Legend. Lecture 20. The Royal Art in a New Form. Berlin, 2nd January 1906.

John the Apostle:

The Book of Revelation. 1:8, 21:6 and 22:13.

Johannes Keppler

Epitome of Copernican Astronomy and Harmonies of the World (1616). Prometheus (3 July 2012)

Ita Wegman:

The Philosopher's Stone in Human Development - February 1927 From 'In the Dawn of Efforts for an Expansion of the Healing Arts' (Natura-Verlag 1956)

Henricus Madathanus (Pseudonym), also Adrian von Mynsicht:

Parabola, ca 1630

Dennis Klocek

The Alchemical Wedding: Christian Rosenkreuz, the Initiate of Misunderstanding. Lindisfarne Books (7 Sept. 2021)

Carl Gustav Jung

Dreams. Routledge (19 Sept. 1985)

Paracelsus (Pseudonym), also Theophrastus von Hohenheim

Complete works. Volumes I-IV. Ed.: Arschner, G., Fischer Verlag, Jena 1926-32

H. Lawrence Bond

Nicholas of Cusa, Selected Spiritual Writings, trans., Paulist Press, New York, 1997, 335-336

Peter Gruenewald

Mastering Life: Rosicrucian and Magical Techniques for Achieving Your Life's Goals. Clairview Books (17 Oct. 2022).

Gold and the Philosopher's Stone. Treating Chronic Physical and mental Illness with Mineral Remedies. Temple Lodge Publishing (3 May 2002)

The Quiet Heart. Putting Stress in its Place. Floris Books; Illustrated edition (23 July 2007)

Printed in France by Amazon
Brétigny-sur-Orge, FR

20158684R00114